FIRST
GARDEN

How to Get Started in

Northeast Gardening

Darrell Trout

with Rob Proctor

FIRST
GARDEN

How to Get Started in
Northeast
Gardening

Darrell Trout

with Rob Proctor

Cool Springs Press
Nashville, Tennessee

Published by Cool Springs Press,
a Division of Thomas Nelson, Inc.,
P. O. Box 141000, Nashville, Tennessee 37214.

Library of Congress Cataloging-in-Publication Data
Trout, Darrell.
   How to get started in northeast gardening / Darrell Trout, with Rob Proctor.
      p. cm. — (First garden)
   Includes bibliographical references and index.
   ISBN 1-59186-159-4
   1. Gardening—Northeastern States. 2. Plants, Ornamental—Northeastern States.
I. Proctor, Rob. II. Title. III. Series.
   SB453.2.N82T76 2005
   635.9'0974--dc22

                                                        2004030927

Printed in the United States of America
10 9 8 7 6 5 4 3 2 1

Book Development & Project Management: Marlene Blessing, Marlene Blessing Editorial
Copyediting: Melanie Stafford
Design & Formatting: Constance Bollen, cb graphics
First Garden Series Consultant: Darrell Trout
Map: Bill Kersey, Kersey Graphics

FRONT COVER: Images clockwise from upper left corner are lily 'Casa Blanca' (CB), obedient plant (TE), purple coneflower (JP), and hosta (JP). All photographs are copyright © Cathy Wilkinson Barash (CB), Tom Eltzroth (TE), and Jerry Pavia (JP) as noted.

BACK COVER: A mix of roses, lavender, yarrow, daisies, and coreopsis. Photograph copyright © David Winger.

Cool Springs Press books may be purchased in bulk
for educational, business, fundraising, or sales promotional use.
For information, please email SpecialMarkets@ThomasNelson.com.

Visit the Thomas Nelson Web site at www.ThomasNelson.com
and the Cool Springs Press Web site at www.coolspringspress.net.

To my great-grandmother,

whose cottage garden brimmed

with fragrant peonies, pinks, and roses

and who planted the gardening seed

in my psyche.

And to those picking up trowels for the first time—

start now, have fun, and play in the dirt!

Oak leaf hydrangea (*Hydrangea quercifolia*)

ACKNOWLEDGMENTS

To Marlene Blessing, the First Garden series creator, editor, my friend and mentor, who invited me to the party and kept me on task.

To DiAnn Lisica, novice gardener, who read the manuscript and made sure it helped rather than confused the beginning gardener.

And to my wife, Geri, who asked last week, "Is that book done yet?"

FIRST GARDEN

NORTHEAST
GARDENING

SECTION 2 / 65

Your Northeast Garden
by Darrell Trout

———

PHOTOGRAPHY CREDITS

Liz Ball: 75, 88, 106 top and bottom, 110 bottom, 119 top, 124, 131, 159

Pegi Ballister-Howells: 65 upper right, 123 bottom

Cathy Wilkinson Barash: 15 lower left, 147

Karen Bussolini: 166

Conard-Pyle Company/Star® Roses: 15 lower right, 114 bottom, 117

Tom Eltzroth: 15 upper left, 65 lower left, 65 lower right, 76 left, 91, 95 bottom, 100, 103 top and bottom, 105, 113, 127, 132 top and bottom, 140, 149 bottom, 150, 153, 154 top, 156, 159

Dency Kane: 2, 78, 81, 93, 144, 154 bottom

Charles Mann: 99 top

Jerry Pavia: 6, 15 upper right, 65 upper left, 67, 68, 95 top, 96, 109, 110 top, 114 top, 119 bottom, 120, 128 bottom, 135, 137 top

Rob Proctor: 17, 18, 21, 24, 25, 27, 29, 30, 31, 33 upper left and 33 upper right, 34, 35, 37, 38, 40, 42, 44, 45, 48, 49, 51, 57, 59, 63, 137 bottom, 142 bottom

Felder Rushing: 73, 82 left, 138, 142 top

Darrell Trout: 16, 66, 76 right, 82 right, 99 bottom, 128 top, 149 top, 161

Andre Viette: 123 top

David Winger: 5, 87

For First-Time Gardeners Everywhere

No matter what part of the country you live in, it is possible to create a vibrant garden that adds beauty to your home and to your *life*. The First Garden series of books are meant for anyone who is just beginning to create his or her first garden. To someone who is new to gardening, a successful, thriving garden may seem like a feat to which only professionals and those with green thumbs can aspire. However, with a clear introduction to the basics—understanding your region (climate, soil, and topography); knowing the plants that grow best in your region; applying good design principles; and learning how to maintain and boost your garden's performance—you will quickly be able to start a garden. And do so with confidence! Before you know it, you may be sharing your garden dos and don'ts with your neighbor across the way.

In Section One of the book, you'll find easy-to-understand guidance to help you master the basics. As you read through this general introduction to gardening, written by nationally recognized garden expert Rob Proctor, you'll see photographs that aren't necessarily specific to your region. These are used to illustrate a design principle, technique, planting combination, or other important concept. Don't worry that your region has been forgotten! The entire final portion of the book, Section Two, is exclusively devoted to gardening specifics for your home turf. In addition to learning such things as how to improve your soil, when to plant bulbs, how to prune a tree or bush, and what kind of troubleshooting you may need to do, you'll also get a complete list of 50 sure-fire plants for your garden. Our regional garden experts have carefully selected these plants to enable you to have the best start possible as you begin what we hope will become a lifetime activity for you.

Like most pursuits, gardening takes time and patience to master. The First Garden books are designed to give you a reliable, can't-miss start. In addition to learning how to grow plants in your region, you will discover the process of turning your landscape into a beautiful, nurturing extension of your home. Even if you are beginning with only a few containers of plants on your deck or patio, you'll soon find that gardening rewards you with colors and scents that make your environment infinitely more satisfying.

With this book as your portable "garden expert," you can begin a great new adventure, knowing that you have friendly, clear advice that will keep you on the garden path. Most of all, we want to welcome you to gardening!

The Editors at Cool Springs Press

USDA Cold Hardiness Zone Map

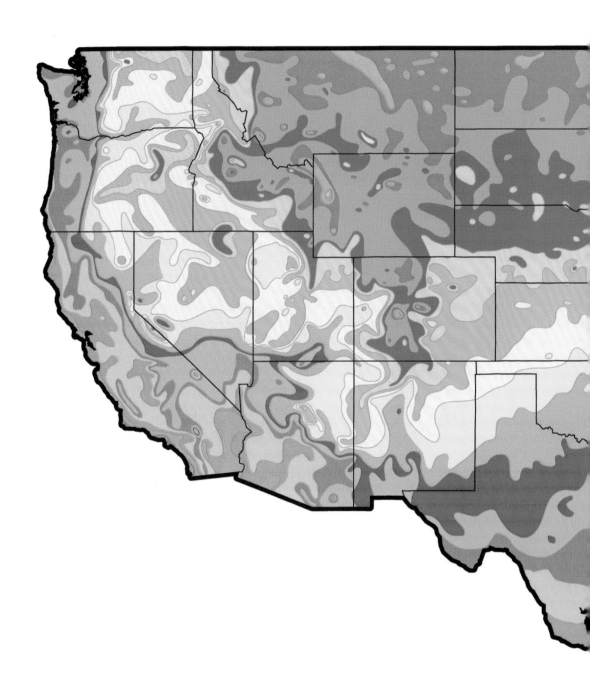

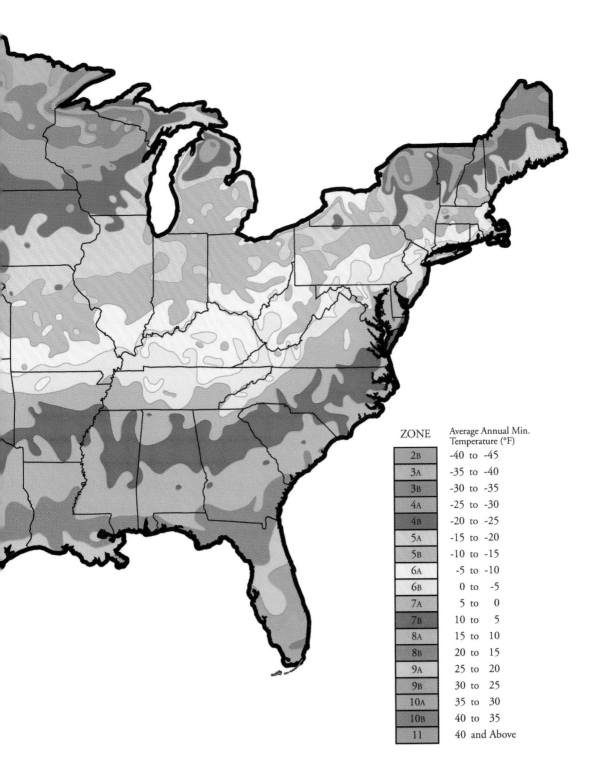

ZONE	Average Annual Min. Temperature (°F)	
2B	-40 to -45	
3A	-35 to -40	
3B	-30 to -35	
4A	-25 to -30	
4B	-20 to -25	
5A	-15 to -20	
5B	-10 to -15	
6A	-5 to -10	
6B	0 to -5	
7A	5 to 0	
7B	10 to 5	
8A	15 to 10	
8B	20 to 15	
9A	25 to 20	
9B	30 to 25	
10A	35 to 30	
10B	40 to 35	
11	40 and Above	

❀ Section 1

Your First Garden

Your first garden is unique. It might start as a blank canvas at a newly built house, without so much as a blade of grass. Or it could be an established landscape that you wish to make your own. Your approach will depend on your scenario. Your first garden might not even include land at the moment; perhaps, if you're an urban dweller, you've decided to garden on a rooftop or balcony.

Making a new garden is complex, intimidating, engrossing, and thrilling. It's all about color, design, and placement. Our visions dance before our eyes like sugar plum fairies. We're capable once again of that magic we used to know as children. My friend Wendy just started her first garden, and I helped her with some planning and took her shopping for plants. We filled her SUV and she rushed home to plant. She called me to say she was "enthralled in the madness" and some of our initial planning went out the window as her creative juices flowed. Good for her!

It would be rare if a garden turned out exactly as planned. However, countless TV makeover shows lead us to believe that this can happen. We see the plan, then some fast-motion digging and planting, then the finished project and the dazed surprise of the happy homeowner. This

---

Visions spring to life in the form of satiny Iceland poppies, coral bells, and tiny 'Zing Rose' dianthus

Lush and romantic, this garden features roses scrambling onto a wagon wheel, coral Jupiter's beard, spikes of fireweed, and a pink skirt of Mexican evening primrose.

all happens in the course of several days, boiled down to less than a 30-minute show. But then what? What happens to the new garden afterward?

Don't get me wrong. I like these shows and often get good design ideas from them. But without a follow-up, we don't have any idea what became of the transformation we've just witnessed. Did the owner water enough? Too much? Did the plants get enough sun? Did those vines cover the new trellis that hides that ugly garage wall? Did the perennials fill in like a soft carpet around the new pond? Or did bindweed and thistle sprout everywhere, choke out the new plants, and return the area to its former dilapidated, dismal state?

My own first garden was poorly planned, badly designed, chock-full of mistakes—and absolutely wonderful. Filled with boundless enthusiasm and unwarranted confidence from growing up in a gardening family, I blundered my way within a few years to creating a garden that was the subject of glamorous layouts in three magazines. In the process, I devoured hundreds of gardening books, subscribed to every horticultural magazine and newsletter I could find, visited every public and private garden I could, and lost twenty pounds.

I planted, transplanted, divided, amended, pruned, mulched, whacked, hacked, hoed, pinched, seeded, and fertilized until my thumb turned green. Making your first garden can be one of the most stimulating and creative experiences of your life. It might also be frustrating, confusing, and occasionally heartbreaking. It all depends on how you do it. You can take small steps or giant leaps. I'm a leaper myself, but I appreciate the cautious, practical approach, of which I'm incapable. The kind of people who plan meticulously might need a big sketch pad and several notebooks (you're probably mentally planning a shopping trip for this purpose at exactly 4:45 P.M. tomorrow afternoon). And it wouldn't hurt to construct a storyboard (borrow the bulletin board from your kid's room) of pictures and articles clipped from magazines, photos from friends' and public gardens, and even key words you want to remember as overriding themes. "Romantic," "lush," "bountiful," and "low-maintenance" don't go in the same sentence, by the way. But we'll talk about realistic maintenance later.

> **My own first garden was poorly planned, badly designed, chock-full of mistakes— and absolutely wonderful.** ✿

Your notebooks can start to fill with color swatches; plant "wish lists"; clippings from the paper; brochures from fence, irrigation, and patio furniture companies; and preliminary budget figures. This might sound a bit like decorating a living room (and indeed your garden will be a "living" room), but there's a difference. With an indoor space you actually reach a point where it's considered finished. With a garden—as an evolving place—it's never completely finished, just done "for now." A garden that doesn't change is not only impossible, but I guarantee you would find it boring.

■ Discovering Your Inner Gardener

When you begin to garden, there are so many considerations it's tough to know where to start. So let's start with you. Do you like gardening work? That means watering, fertilizing, digging, planting, pruning, and all that? Not to mention the dreaded "W" word—weeding. Unlike tennis or ballet, gardening doesn't require any particular talents or physical attributes such as grace or brute strength. It just takes industriousness. People who like to keep house or fix cars, for example, may make fine gardeners, because the plans of attack to get the job done are similar.

Gardening is the number-one pastime in our country. Perhaps not everyone practices it to a refined degree, but this does mean that, in general, we enjoy the pleasures of working in the soil and raising flowers and vegetables. Your garden is what you make it. You'll be surprised how quickly you'll pick up the knowledge and skills to make yours beautiful and productive. Gardening is part art and part science, so there's room for everybody—right- or left-brainers— to get into the act. A friend of mine once called gardening the "slowest of the performing arts." You're the director and the plants you grow are the stars and supporting players.

As the director of your horticultural extravaganza (as well as the set designer, head writer, and entire technical crew), start with your vision. Some people might begin with a low-budget home movie, and others envision an epic blockbuster. Our inspirations come from many sources— childhood memories, books and magazines, and travels. And since I've drawn an analogy to the movies, let's acknowledge that many of us find inspiration on the silver screen as well. Sometimes

I feel my garden resembles the one in *The Secret Garden*. Before the children cleaned it up. (By the way, those were remarkably skilled kids, outperforming a crew of at least 20 landscapers.)

■ Blueprints for the Garden

As you plan your garden and its "rooms," take a look at what you've got—at ground level and below. City and suburban dwellers often live in a house that sits on a square, flat lot. Even a rooftop or balcony gardener usually deals with a level rectangular space. On the other hand, perhaps you live amidst hills, valleys, embankments, or even streams or ponds on your property. Your nearest neighbor may be feet or miles away.

It's probably time to clarify the difference between a landscape and a garden. Although the two are connected, there are some differences. A landscape applies to everything on the property, but most specifically trees, shrubs, and hardscape (walkways, walls, driveways, decks, patios). A landscape may include "garden areas" as a part of its overall scheme. The traditional American landscape typically features a lot of lawn, "foundation plantings" of shrubs that hug the house, and various trees placed for shade. It's a nice, familiar picture, perhaps with a strip of geraniums or petunias bordering the walk. Or maybe there's a flowerbed skirting the row of junipers or yews lined up under the eaves of the house.

The footprint of your house, any outbuildings, and adjacent buildings define your site. One way or the other, you may wish to make a blueprint of your property to draw and dream upon. It doesn't need to be exactly to scale (or even blue). I wouldn't even recommend doing much detailed planning on it since one-dimensional blueprints rarely translate into beautiful three-dimensional gardens. Just use it to familiarize yourself with all the features of your existing site (or lack of them) and for the placement of present and future walkways, driveways, patios, walls, trees, and specific garden areas or features. These could be things such as herb, cutting, or vegetable gardens as well as borders, ponds, play areas, and so forth. I often sketch on a legal pad to help me plan or revamp an area. (I once designed a friend's garden on a cocktail napkin, but that's another story that taught me I need a bigger piece of paper.)

If you picture creating a garden that is more unique, you won't need to exclude any of these traditional elements. Instead, you'll treat them somewhat differently and focus more directly on flowers and vegetables and their relationships to everything else on the property. In this scenario, there's a nearly constant, hands-on relationship between you and the plants, far beyond a weekly mowing or annual hedge trimming. If you really like plants, you can transform any static landscape into an active garden.

■ About Soil

What color is your thumb? People who meet me often feel obliged to apologize for their black thumbs. "I kill everything," they tell me. There's no such thing as a black thumb. Everybody can garden. Plants—like pets—need water, food, a suitable place to live, and occasional grooming. Green thumbs aren't born, they're made. The origin of the term stems from the fact that gardeners put excessive wear and tear on their thumbs and forefingers. As they pinch petunias or pull pigweed, the green sap stains eventually become engrained for most of the gardening season. My thumb's not a classic green but more of a dirty olive tone. Let's not mention my knuckles and nails, which are accented by various cuts, scrapes, and punctures.

You don't need to ruin your hands. Sensible glove-wearing gardeners still deserve the title green thumb. You can earn it, too. Learn the basics and build on those, just the way you'd approach any new pastime such as cooking, tennis, sewing, or carpentry.

Okay, former black thumbs: get started. Dig a spadeful of soil. (If you're a rooftop or balcony gardener, skip this and go buy some potting soil.) Squeeze a handful. Does it stick together into a mud ball? You have clay. That's most of us. If the ball of soil falls apart, you've got sand. It's an easier soil to dig, but dries out more quickly. If you're extremely lucky, you're blessed with rich, black "Iowa cornfield" soil that gardeners crave (in which case you're probably reading this in Iowa). Don't worry. Both clay and sandy soil can be amended to grow some traditional plants. On the other hand, a good many plants are so adaptable that they'll grow well in almost any kind of soil.

Once you've done some experimenting, you can decide what—if anything—you want to do to your soil. I actually don't amend soil, but grow what wants to grow in that soil. I've often read or seen experts who recommend a soil test. I've never done one. I wouldn't have a clue what it meant if I had 100 parts magnesium

> **Green thumbs aren't born, they're made.**

A garden planted in unimproved clay soil, rarely irrigated, supports many drought-tolerant perennials including varieties of penstemons and bright Jupiter's beard.

per million. Unless you suspect that your soil has an actual problem (such as being missing after the builders finished the house) or has some sort of contamination, I can't imagine the value of a test unless you want to grow rare alpine plants from Switzerland. Even if your soil has been pounded and pulverized by heavy equipment, you don't need a soil test to tell you it's been compacted and that with just a little more pressure will turn into diamonds. Most people have the kind of soil that everybody else in their neighborhood has. What's growing there? Does it look healthy? If the trees are dying and lawns are sickly, don't get a soil test—call the Environmental Protection Agency.

Your soil will actually teach you as you go along what it's capable of doing. It may not support absolutely every type of plant you might want to grow (I'll never have blueberries), but odds are it has plenty of potential. For extreme sand or clay, you may decide to amend or alter your soil or bring in topsoil for plants with specific needs (I would need to create an acidic bog to grow blueberries). But first explore what your soil can do before you begin a wholesale radical makeover that will forever alter its composition.

Don't just start adding ingredients willy-nilly. Many books often recommend adding lime to the soil as a matter of course. The assumption is that most plants do best if grown in a soil that is about neutral on the pH scale. This advice may be all well and good in Cleveland or Boston where the soil pH is on the acid side, for the lime would reduce the acidity. But for gardeners in the West, which generally has an alkaline soil, the lime would be a waste of time, like giving "The Rock" a gym membership for his birthday. The point is to be familiar with your soil type and composition, but don't stress about it.

■ Weather and Gardening Zones

Before you start thinking about planting, determine in which climate zone you live. The U.S. Department of Agriculture (USDA) issues a detailed map, found at the front of this book, that illustrates these zones throughout the country. Based primarily on average minimum temperatures, the map helps you determine which plants will survive in your area. Almost all the plants you buy will be rated as to the zones where they are hardy, meaning where they'll survive an average winter. Most nurseries in your region only carry plants that are appropriate to it. But if you purchase plants online or by mail, you should be aware of your zone so you don't end up planting a tropical palm in Minnesota.

> Many gardeners expand their options by clever gardening known as "zone denial."
> ✿

IN THE ZONE

The USDA climate zone map is a good aid in helping you decide what to grow, but it has its limitations. For example, it doesn't take into account rainfall, humidity, and, most importantly, high temperatures. These factors also affect plant survival. You'll find that Chicago, Denver, and Hartford are all categorized as zone 5, but their actual growing conditions vary considerably. Rainfall, humidity, and summer heat—as well as soil type—may play as great a role in plant performance as winter low temperatures. Southern gardeners sometimes find that plants considered hardy for their zone won't thrive in their summer heat or need a colder winter dormancy than southern climes provide. Tulips are a case in point. It all sounds terribly complicated, but as you visit local nurseries and gardens, you'll get the hang of it. You'll soon start to get a grasp of what wants to grow in your area.

MICROCLIMATES

Adhering to the zone designations may help you play it safe, but many gardeners expand their options by clever gardening known as "zone denial." After all, plants can't read. If they receive the conditions that allow them to thrive, they will. This is where knowing your garden site intimately is vital. Throughout it there are "microclimates," little pockets formed by topography, fences, trees, and walls. Your house offers the most differentiations. Southern and western exposures are usually hotter and sunnier; northern and eastern exposures, cooler and shadier. The placement of trees can moderate or enhance these conditions.

A hill or outcropping may afford at least two distinct microclimates in much the same way as your house does. Lower areas tend to be cooler and, because cold air sinks, often freeze earlier than higher ground, as well as collecting and holding moisture. Knowing this helps you to position plants that prefer either well-drained soil (on a slope) or moist soil (in a hog wallow). Both air and water drain in the same manner on a large scale. Cold air often "flows" along streams and rivers, making low-lying areas "frost pockets" and higher ground "banana belts." If you're in a low-lying area, there's not much you can do about this, of course, except to be more cautious about setting out tender plants in spring or protecting them in the fall. If you're on a hilltop, you can just feel smug. But hilltops may get fierce winds (in gardening, there's a plus and minus to every condition). Knowing the direction of the prevailing wind helps prevent mistakes as well; otherwise you may be staking your delphiniums with rebar.

Paving and foundations, as well as rocks and rock outcrops also affect plant performance, either for better or worse, depending on the plant. Some plants revel in the extra heat from driveways, walkways, and foundations, and others can't stand baking. Many plants also like to get their roots beneath rocks and paving not only because of the extra heat, but because the mass of the stone moderates the surrounding temperatures by virtue of its slow heating and cooling. Rock gardeners exploit these possibilities to the max, with every nook and cranny offering a potential microclimate for a special plant.

Wherever you live, you can create a beautiful garden. Gardeners often envy others who live in different climates, usually because of particular plants that grow beautifully in that environment. By all means, experiment to see if you can achieve similar results. But don't get hung up on a certain flower that has little intention of performing for you. Yes, I've made attempts to grow azaleas and rhododendrons that I admire in friends' gardens in Virginia. And failed. So I'm content to visit them in spring and enjoy their good fortune. They come to see me, too, to admire western specialties that their gardens can't accommodate successfully, like prickly poppies and penstemons.

Although we often equate an abundance of moisture with successful gardening, it's only because the spectacular gardens in rainy regions get most of the good press. Lovely, original gardens are found within every region of our country. They are filled with the plants that want to grow there. Some may be native wildflowers, and others may originate in areas around the

A rock-terraced slope provides good drainage and extra heat for purple verbena, agave, and ice plants, with a backdrop of golden black-eyed Susans.

world with similar climate and soil. Fortunately for all of us, there's an enormous pool of plants that offer amazing abilities to adapt to a wide spectrum of conditions. Like our country itself, your new garden is likely to become a melting pot of flowers and styles from many lands—with your very own personal stamp.

■ Plant Names: Why Latin?

There's no escaping it. You need a little Latin—not much, but a little. Every living thing, animal and plant, is classified scientifically using a system that speaks Latin. To keep the millions of distinct forms of life in some sort of reasonable order, they all have a scientific name, much like our first and last names. It avoids duplication. If you looked in the phone book under Mary Jones or Bob Smith, you understand how confusing it could get if we just called plants "bluebell" or "daisy."

Most people know more scientific plant names than they think. Even non-gardeners are familiar with *chrysanthemum, geranium, lobelia, dahlia, crocus, phlox, gardenia, verbena, begonia,* and *petunia*. Others aren't much of a stretch, such as *rosa* for rose, *lilium* for lily, *tulipa* for tulip, or *hyacinthus* for hyacinth.

Within any genus of plants or animals there are individual species. Let's start with people. We all belong to the genus *Homo*, meaning human. And our species is *sapiens*, meaning wise or intelligent. We belong to the classification "intelligent human." We don't need to draw this distinction very often since the rest of the members of our genus are extinct. *Homo erectus* was "standing man," who apparently could walk upright but wasn't known for his brain. The traits of particular plants are often noted in their species name, called the specific epitaph, such as their color, habit, size, leaf shape, their resemblance to something else, what habitat they grow in, their country or region of origin, or something like that. They don't always make a whole lot of sense. Sometimes they honor a botanist who first discovered them or somebody to whom the discoverer wanted to suck up. After all, who wouldn't want a plant named for them? Most plants were named hundreds of years ago, although new discoveries occasionally crop up in rain forests.

When plant breeders get involved, plants acquire yet another name. Say that you, as a plant breeder, cross two different species to create a brand-new offspring with distinctly different characteristics from the two parents. Or say that, as a sharp-eyed gardener or nursery owner, you spot an unusual variation in an otherwise uniform batch of plants. What do you do? Name it, of course, for your wife, husband, mother, daughter, or a celebrity you admire. Or if you're more creative, you go for something more lyrical or amusing. That's why we have *Anemone* x *hybrida* 'Honorine Jobert' (named for the guy's daughter), the hybrid tea rose 'Dolly Parton' (a voluptuous flower), and the self-descriptive petunia 'Purple Wave' (the color really flows). I've always hoped to create a new color of the trailing annual *Bacopa* and call it 'Cabana'. The gardening world is waiting. . . .

Penstemon fanciers need to know the scientific names of pink *Penstemon palmeri* and purple *P. strictus*.

> **When it comes to pronunciation, don't stress. Latin is a dead language. It's nobody's native tongue.**

As for the scientific names, we don't use them very much except for perennials. Not too many people say *quercus* instead of oak or *curcubita* instead of squash (unless they're really, really snobbish). Whenever a common name will do, use it. Most gardeners—in my opinion—should just talk about daylilies, Russian sage, and yarrow without trying to tie their tongues around *hemerocallis, perovskia,* or *achillea*. But in some cases, especially when you're talking about a genus with a whole bunch of species, and you need to get specific about which one, the only way is to use Latin. There are hundreds of varieties of *penstemon*, for example. These lovely western wildflowers, commonly called beardtongue (yuck), range from tall scarlet *Penstemon barbatus* to mat-forming blue *Penstemon virens*. Then there's pretty orange *P. pinifolius*, lovely pink *P. palmeri*, and wispy white *P. ambiguas*. If you get into penstemons, you gotta speak the lingo.

When it comes to pronunciation, don't stress. Latin is a dead language. It's nobody's native tongue. Do your best with this cumbersome old language. And if someone dares to correct your pronunciation of a name, just stare him or her down coolly and say, "Oh, that's the way I used to say it." This implies that you have been hanging out with more knowledgeable gardeners than they have and you must obviously be right.

Sort out the easy mispronunciations before you go to the nursery so you don't have them snickering behind your back. *Cotoneaster* is "ka-tone-ee-aster" not "cotton Easter." I'd say flowering tobacco for *nicotiana*, but if you must, pronounce it "ni-coh-she-anna" not "nikko-teen-a." Avoid *aquilegia* ("ah-qui-lee-ja" not "a-quill-a-gee-a"), and just say columbine instead.

■ Plant Types

TREES: GARDEN ELDERS

All this talk of sites, soils, and climates brings us to the basic business of knowing and growing plants. Plants have evolved to fill niches created by geography and topography. Trees tower above everything (sort of like carnivores on the food chain). They're tough and long-lived. Any tree planted today will, with care, likely outlive any of us, so its placement is the most critical of any plant you put in the soil. Trees need space. With their specific needs varying by species, they need enough room between them and your house, each other, power lines, and features like that. In most cities, the office of forestry offers guidelines and regulations on tree planting. Street trees especially must be placed so as to not block sight lines at intersections or to interfere with power lines and street lights. If you get it wrong, some city employee will probably pay you a visit. Some kinds and types of trees are even forbidden because they are brittle and are prone to breaking under snow and ice or from wind, which endangers cars and passersby. Multistemmed trees such as redbuds or dogwoods are often prohibited for planting along streets since they can block the views at intersections. Most drivers can see around a single trunk tree adequately, but a big mass of foliage is dangerous.

Breaks in the canopy of trees allows beds of perennials and ornamental grasses to flourish in this well-conceived plan.

Trees differ in many ways. Evergreens hold their leaves (called needles if the tree is a spruce, pine, fir, or cypress) throughout the year, while deciduous trees drop their leaves in fall and grow new ones in spring. In frost-free climates, some trees hold their leaves throughout the year, while others still go through a seasonal renewal. At least two kinds of "evergreen" tree, the larch and bald cypress, go dormant in fall and drop their needles. There's an infamous tale in my city of a park maintenance crew who, thinking that it had died, cut down a prized bald cypress that was just in the bald phase of its normal cycle.

All trees flower. Some do it in spectacular fashion, while others are barely noticed except by allergy sufferers. Bees and other insects usually pollinate trees with big, showy, and scented flowers, such as fruit trees. Most other trees rely on the wind to blow about their massive amounts of pollen, which is precisely why spring can be so miserable for some of us.

Most trees have a single main trunk, and most deciduous trees create an interlocking canopy of branches. Trunks of every tree should always be respected and protected. While appearing to be the strongest part of the tree, the trunk is also the most vulnerable. Just beneath the bark is the lifeline of the tree, called the cambium layer, the vascular system that supports the tree the way our veins and arteries support us. When bark is damaged, that damage is usually irreversible, and the limbs on that side of the tree will often die. Even something as insignificant as a weed whacker can damage or kill a tree.

Tree roots need respect and protection, too. Compaction of the soil above the roots is to be avoided as this suffocates them and inhibits their ability to absorb water. The roots that do most of the work of searching for food and water, called feeder roots, are usually at and beyond the shady circle cast by the tree at high noon. This is called the drip line, because rain splashes from leaf to leaf, keeping the area directly beneath relatively dry. Remember that it doesn't do much good to water a tree right at the trunk since its feeder roots are many feet away.

WOODY PLANTS: SPACE AND CARE

Trees are durable because they're made of wood. This is either patently obvious or extremely profound, but I thought it needed to be said. Other woody plants—call them shrubs or bushes, it doesn't matter—are structured like trees. They can also be deciduous or evergreen, but their main similarity is their strong, woody constitution. All the considerations you give to a tree in placement and care apply to shrubs. One of the chronic mistakes that plague American gardeners is to crowd shrubs and not give them enough room to develop. This leads to much whacking and hacking, resulting in distorted, weird-looking bushes, often represented by the classic "light bulb" trim job. I know you've seen it. You've probably also driven past houses that have almost completely disappeared behind rampaging junipers whose growth habits the owners underestimated. There's a hilarious example in my neighborhood where the people neglected to read the tags when they planted cone-shaped junipers in front of their picture windows. Eventually, the view disappeared as the trees grew higher than the house. The owners then decided to trim all the branches below the roofline, leaving thick bare trunks with little "Christmas trees" perched upon them. I chuckle every time I drive by, but there's a lesson in that for all of us.

Most shrubs we grow in our gardens are either selected for their evergreen nature (often for winter interest) or for their flowers. A few, such as holly, are grown primarily for their handsome berries. Almost all flowering shrubs bloom on "old" wood, meaning only branches a year or more old will produce flowers. Keep in mind that if you do prune or trim (shrubs usually need much less grooming than we think), it should be done only right after they've finished blooming. Otherwise you'll be cutting off your next years' display.

ROSES: TENDER OR TOUGH

Roses are certainly the most popular of the shrubs. Novice gardeners want to grow them in the worst way. First-time rose growers envision huge bouquets of long-stemmed tea roses on their dining room tables. It's a nice dream, but those roses you received on Valentine's Day were greenhouse grown in supporting cages to keep their stems straight and long. And the bushes never experienced arctic winters or Saharan heat. Yours probably will.

Let's get realistic about roses. You'll have some for cutting, but don't get any ideas about opening your own flower shop. Wherever you garden, you can successfully grow hundreds of varieties of roses. Just don't get hung up on the hybrid teas at the beginning. Just as rewarding are the old-fashioned shrub roses, climbers, floribundas, and the so-called landscape roses and carpet roses. Most thrive with a minimum of care and some are even drought tolerant.

Shrub roses say romance in the garden. With their graceful, arching canes laden with sweet blooms, they conjure nostalgic visions of castles and cottages. Superb performers, they seldom, if ever, suffer from pests or diseases beyond an aphid or two (easily dispatched with a soapy spray). Widely grown across much of the nation are the classic early bloomers such as 'Persian

Yellow', 'Austrian Copper', and 'Harrison's Yellow'. The red-leaf rose, *Rosa glauca*, takes the prize as the most adaptable shrub rose. It will thrive in conditions from sun to part shade, clay to sand, and wet to dry. Pretty little single pink flowers grace the unusual leaves, blue-gray on top with maroon red underneath.

These large shrub roses can often be found in older neighborhoods where they put on spectacular early displays. Young shrub roses are like gawky teenagers, irregular and awkward looking. Give them space and time to fulfill their promise. Some people avoid planting these classics because they bloom only once each season. That's unfair. After all, I've never heard anyone complain because his or her lilacs, tulips, or lilies bloom only once a year.

Some shrub roses do bloom persistently, even in heat. The *rugosa* hybrids are simply wonderful. If I had to choose just one, it would be 'Therese Bugnet' (pronounced "boon-yay"). On bushes 4' by 5', its glossy green foliage supports full, pink flowers with the perfect "old rose" perfume. I'm also entranced by 'Golden Wings', an upright shrub type that grows to 4' or 5' tall. Its huge, single amber yellow flowers are accented by orange stamens and carry a soft fragrance. For an arbor or trellis, the classic ruby red 'Blaze' can't be beat, while pale pink 'New Dawn' is the stuff of fairy tales. Speaking of which, 'The Fairy' is a dainty but tough little shrub about 3' by 3' with nonstop clusters of satin pink blooms. It's beautiful with lavender or catmint as a "skirt" (most roses are lovely coupled with these plants). All these roses grow well in most regions, but there are certainly regional favorites that you can visit at local municipal gardens. Look

> Wherever you garden, you can successfully grow hundreds of varieties of roses.

Adobe-toned yarrow and a flurry of snow daisies enhance the much-admired classic hybrid tea rose 'Peace.'

Vines are really just shrubs with a posture problem. 🌹

for ones that demonstrate unusual vigor and clean, disease-free leaves. Also keep in mind how much room you want to devote to each bush. Can you accommodate the big boys, or are you best with the little guys?

Other compact varieties that perform tirelessly are the Meidiland series in white, coral, reds, and pinks. Easy and prolific, their single or double flowers fit in effortlessly with perennials such as meadow sage, pincushion flowers, catmints, snow daisies, and yarrow. Most roses—to my mind—look their best planted informally rather than regimented in rows. Hybrid tea roses benefit enormously when surrounded by casual companions that enhance their charms and disguise their weaknesses. To keep the advice short and sweet: plant roses in sun, keep them evenly moist, feed regularly, and prune in spring. I'm fond of a number of hybrid tea roses, but my favorite is the elegant cream and pink 'Peace'. This classic rose, bred in France just before World War II, survived because its breeder shipped a single cutting to a friend in America just before the Nazis invaded. The rest of the roses were destroyed, but 'Peace' endured. Just one of its flowers, floating in a bowl, is all any rose lover needs.

VINES: BEAUTIFUL CLIMBERS

Vines are really just shrubs with a posture problem. They've found a special niche in nature where they rely on their neighbors for support. The ultimate in social climbers, they cling and twine their way to ever-greater heights. Since they are lovely, we forgive them and give them fences, arbors, and trellises on which to grow and flower. Some enchant us with their flowers—clematis, honeysuckle, and wisteria—and others with their foliage—ivy and Virginia creeper. Grapes mean jelly, juice, and wine, and hops are a vital ingredient in beer. I've never made homemade wine or beer, but both grapes and hops make beautiful, albeit rambunctious, additions to the garden. A few very popular vines, such as morning glories and sweet peas, grow, flower, and die in one season, which makes them annuals. We'll talk about them shortly.

A planting of roses and perennials, including pink lupines and white valerian, is peppered with annual bread seed poppies.

PERENNIALS: LASTING PLEASURES

Perennial plants have a completely different strategy for survival than trees and shrubs. When cold weather hits, they retreat underground and wait out winter with their root systems. They return "perennially" each spring. Don't confuse "perennial" with "immortal," however, as some

**Annuals in concert—glowing pink 'First Love' dianthus scores with
blue and white forms of mealy-cup sage.**

perennials run their course in just a few years. Others live to a very old age, such as peonies and daylilies. Since about the last quarter of the twentieth century, most Americans have based the bulk of their gardens around perennials. Just as hemlines go up and down and lapels go wide and then skinny, gardens go through periods of what's in and out. At the moment and for the foreseeable future, perennials figure prominently in most gardens. With trees and shrubs as the backdrop and structure of the garden, perennials take center stage. They're valued for their diversity, toughness, longevity, and—above all—beauty. A wonderful trend in American gardening today is to value every sort of plant and use it to best advantage. While Victorians didn't have much use for perennials, preferring showy, hothouse-raised annuals, we've come to embrace all kinds of plants regardless of their life cycles.

ANNUALS: COLORFUL ADDITIONS

When we picture annuals, we think of those vibrant, tempting flowers bursting out of their six-packs every spring at garden centers, supermarkets, and home improvement stores. These are the plants we rely on for continuous color all summer long. Usually grown from seed, annuals germinate, grow, flower, set seed, and die in a single season. It's a short, but dazzling life cycle. What's considered an annual depends on where you live. In most northern climates, the annual section includes many tender tropical and subtropical perennials, such as geraniums, that aren't hardy below freezing. My sister in Florida has geraniums older than her ancient cat. So in this category, we're including plants with a single-season life cycle in whichever climate you garden. Your local nursery can help you sort it all out. Many gardeners in cold-winter climates move these tender perennials indoors to save them from year to year.

Most annuals come packaged in handy six-packs or four-packs, but for the impatient, many garden centers offer mature blooming annuals in quart- or gallon-size pots. These, of course, come with higher price tags, but presumably are worth it for those who want instant gratification. A number of annuals aren't very suitable for six-packs, and grow best if sown directly in the ground. You'll save money as well as expand your selection if you learn to grow plants from seed. To build your confidence, start with the easy ones like sunflowers and marigolds.

Annuals prove themselves invaluable in a new garden because they grow to full size quickly. While everything else—trees, shrubs, and perennials—put down roots for the long haul, annuals fill the gaps and encourage the new gardener. But they're much more than gap-fillers. Even as the rest of the garden takes off, leave room for the gorgeous gaiety that annuals provide. I'd never want to go through a season without the brilliant blossoms of California poppies, moss roses, larkspurs, zinnias, or salvias. Annuals truly shine in container gardens as well. As mentioned previously, several vines are annual in nature. Among the most popular are morning glories, sweet peas, hyacinth beans, sweet potato vines, canary creepers, and climbing nasturtiums, not to mention peas and pole beans.

Many annuals that find your garden to their liking may respond by sowing themselves from year to year, making a one-time investment in them a very good one indeed. These "volunteers" can be thinned and transplanted to suit you. Johnny-jump-ups, larkspurs, bachelor's buttons, sweet alyssum, and several kinds of poppy—California, Shirley, corn, and lettuce-leaf—likely will form colonies in your garden. Count yourself lucky.

The care of annuals is as diverse as the plants themselves. Some like constant attention with lots of water and fertilizer. Some prefer benign neglect. Morning glories, cosmos, and nasturtiums—if fed and watered too much—will reward you with jungle-like growth, but deny you their flowers. It's called too much of a good thing.

BULBS: SPRING AND FALL

Bulbs take their preservation to extremes. Spring-flowering bulbs such as tulips and daffodils bide their wintertime underground, plumping themselves up with moisture. As winter retreats, the flowers of the bulb emerge. Sometimes they're a bit ahead of schedule and get caught by late freezes and snowstorms. Don't stress about your tulips, hyacinths, crocuses, daffodils, or snowdrops. They've evolved to bloom at that tricky time when winter and spring wrestle for dominance. They can withstand frost and snow (even if some flower stems snap). If they couldn't, they'd be extinct. If a heavy, wet snow threatens your tulips at the height of perfection, by all means cover them with bushel baskets, buckets, card tables, or whatever sheltering device you have handy. But these early bulbs don't need a blanket to keep them warm; they grow and flower best during the cool, sunny days of spring.

LEFT: Fall-blooming crocus belie the season with their springlike charms, contrasted by reddening plumbago foliage. RIGHT: Late spring-blooming Dutch iris pair attractively with variegated dogwood.

When things heat up, the spring bulbs finish their annual cycle by setting seed, soaking up the sun to provide energy for the next spring, and going through their ugly phase of unkempt, yellowing leaves. The best thing you can do is snap off their seedpods so they don't waste the energy, fertilize the plants to ensure a great display next spring, and ignore the yellowing leaves until they've turned brown. If you cut or pull off the foliage prematurely, you'll likely affect the bulb's ability to turn in a star performance next season. Live with it. By planting the bulbs farther back in beds—rather than right at the edge—emerging perennials will help camouflage the dying bulb leaves.

Summer doesn't spell the end of bulbs. Some even bloom in fall. The term bulb, by the way, refers to the enlarged roots that have evolved over time for each kind of bulbous plant. Some are categorized as true bulbs (tulips and lilies), some as corms (crocuses and gladiolus), some as rhizomes (irises), and others as tubers (dahlias). They all vary in shape and size, but they are all efficient storage containers. And the great thing is that they can sit dormant for months while they zip around the world, arriving at planting time at your neighborhood nursery. Then these hard brown chunks get buried, send out roots, plump up, and emerge above ground to grow and flower. I've always found that wondrous and wonderful.

The summer bulbs may be either hardy or tender, depending, once again, on where you garden. For most people, lilies, irises, and liatris can be treated as perennials. The rest of them—dahlias, cannas, elephant ears, caladiums, and gladiolus—must be dug after frost and their bulbs, corms, rhizomes, and tubers stored over winter.

Startling Flanders poppies seed themselves among an easy-care collection of classic bearded iris that are cut back and divided every four or five years.

I must warn you here about falling into a very bad habit concerning bearded iris. I adore these plants, so I feel protective toward them. Anyway, irises grow quickly, and to keep them healthy and blooming, you need to divide them every four or five years. After they flower in late spring, you dig up a clump and break up the rhizomes into pieces about six inches long with a single "fan" of leaves. You replant each fan right near the soil surface with 6" to 8" between each piece. Now here's the important part: Because the rhizome has a lot of work to do in getting its roots reestablished, you help out by cutting the fan of leaves down by half with scissors. The roots can't support all that top growth. If you follow these directions, you'll grow superb iris. However, never cut back the foliage unless you're transplanting the iris. For some odd reason, millions of Americans think they should go out after these bloom and punish their iris for a job well done by disfiguring the leaves and cutting off half of their system of making food. If I see you've done it, I'll knock on your door and give you a stern lecture. I travel extensively, so don't think you're safe just because you live in Salt Lake City or Sheboygan.

Summer- and autumn-flowering bulbs make amazing contributions to the garden and patio pots. I'm especially fond of cannas, lilies, and dahlias in big pots as exotic, colorful exclamation points on terraces and patios. Often overlooked, fall-blooming bulbs add enchantment to our gardens late in the season. Put a note in your daytimer to buy and plant them in late summer and early fall. It's worth the effort. Fall crocuses bring a touch of spring to our beds and borders even as the backdrop changes to yellow and bronze. Springing from the earth without leaves, these pretty flowers are ideally planted in concert with low-growing ground cover perennials such as thyme, partridge feather, and plumbago. Unusual in their life cycles, these bulbs send up their leaves in spring, soak up the sun, and disappear until their surprise late performance.

HERBS: USEFUL AND BEAUTIFUL

It used to be that the only herbs most folks encountered were lavender in their soaps, some mint in their juleps, and perhaps some parsley garnishing their dinner plates. Thank goodness those days are gone. As we all hunger for a healthier, tastier diet, herbs have become invaluable in our kitchens. We find them in many facets of our lives, from the medicine cabinet to the bathtub and the linen closet. Many people classify herbs as the "useful plants," whether they're used for culinary, cosmetic, medicinal, or household purposes.

An herb garden can be a charming garden room. Alternately, herbs lend themselves to growing in borders or vegetable and cutting gardens as well as pots. One big misconception that you may have heard

> As we all hunger for a healthier, tastier diet, herbs have become invaluable in our kitchens.

An unusual "scare camel" protects a country garden that rivals those in southern France for charm, with its casual mix of lavender, daisies, poppies and ornamental onions.

repeated is that herbs like terrible soil and tough conditions. This, of course, depends on your soil type, but I guess it stems from the fact that many popular cooking herbs come from the Mediterranean region. Oregano, thyme, tarragon, rosemary, lavender, savory, and sage love full sun, don't need much water, and prosper in a mineral-rich, not-too-fluffed-up soil. To some people, that means poor soil; but for most of us, that's what we've got. Other herbs such as basil or ginger like organically rich, moist soil. Herbs display the same diversity as any other group of plants but, in general, are quite adaptable. Many that you wish to grow may thrive happily in a room devoted strictly to them. As you grow and experiment with this fascinating group, your kitchen and home will change forever.

TURF: WISE CARE

One of my summer chores growing up was tending the lawn. I hated it. But I learned what it took to have a healthy lawn with minimal effort (never underestimate an adolescent who'd rather be doing something else). Fertilize and aerate in spring and fall. Dig dandelions by hand the minute they start to bloom. Water during the coolest part of the day. And water infrequently and deeply to encourage the roots to delve deeply in search of water. Roots near the surface burn up. Set the mower blade at the highest level, the better to shade the roots during hot weather.

I've stood by these early findings ever since, and I've always had healthy, resilient lawns with a minimum of crabgrass (which I also hand-dig before it goes to seed) and never an instance of mold, fungus, or the other horrors that seem to plague overwatered grass. An inch of moisture a week is not only sufficient but also advisable for a tough turf that can roll with the punches. If you get moss in parts of your lawn, consider this: perhaps nature is telling you that moss would be more suitable than turf. Some of the most beautiful "lawns" I've seen in New England were made of moss.

I've recently reached a point in my life where I am lawn-free. The recent western drought pushed me over the edge. I don't begrudge anyone else's right to enjoy their lawn for family activities and, perhaps, the pleasure of tending it. Just do it responsibly and wisely to get the most out of your work and water. Many seasoned gardeners I know have little or no lawn. It all starts by expanding the borders by a foot or two. Sometimes a gardening couple will argue about whether this is necessary (husbands tend to treasure the time spent with their lawns), but eventually the border prevails.

As you plan your new garden, you may be starting with nothing more than a lawn. Ask yourself, "Do I really want that responsibility, to maintain a lawn up to the neighborhood standard?" It's work. Flower and vegetable gardening is work, too, but a lot less monotonous, and (in my opinion) infinitely more rewarding. Limiting the size of turf areas reduces water consumption and allows you to better care for what you've got. Eventually, I'd guess, you'll be nibbling away at the edges to make more room for flowers.

GROUND COVERS AND TURF ALTERNATIVES: ALONE OR TOGETHER

While various kinds of turf are the ultimate ground covers, a number of low-growing, low-maintenance perennials can serve much the same purpose. They're not suitable for badminton or dodgeball, but they offer a pretty alternative to the big stretch of green lawn. They're also

A tapestry of ground covers on a rocky slope includes sedums, snow-on-the-mountain, and ice plants, punctuated by flaming Oriental poppies.

---

ideal for slopes, hills, and irregular terrain that may be a challenge to mow. You can choose to plant a single ground cover, such as a moss or thyme. Or you can plant many kinds of ground covers as a tapestry of intertwining colors and textures. The best ground covers for your area will be found at your local nursery. Widely grown kinds include creeping veronica, thyme, brass button, ivy, lily turf (*Liriope*), pachysandra, lamium, vinca, wine cup, partridge feather, creeping baby's breath, mat daisy, Irish and Scottish moss, creeping phlox, hen and chicks, sedum, and ice plant. In addition, many require less water than most lawn grasses and little or no fertilization. And you never need to mow. Your world will become a quieter place.

■ Your Style

Never give up your vision. Style transcends climate. Almost everything is possible, budget and patience permitting. At the same time, consider the region in which you live and its natural landscape, as well as its signature plants—whether native (meaning indigenous) or not—that provide its gardening identity. After all, what's Portland without roses, Phoenix without saguaro cacti, New Orleans without bougainvillea vines, Richmond without dogwood trees, Denver without

> Style transcends climate. Almost everything is possible, budget and patience permitting.

Southwestern gardeners draw on the desert and Native American cultures for inspiration, as strong architectural plants make a bold style statement.

blue spruce, or Washington, D.C., without cherry trees? The gardening heritage of your city or state may be an important factor in determining the style and contents of your garden.

The architecture of your home also figures into that determination. My modest turn-of-the-century cottage would look downright silly with a Louis XIV clipped ornamental garden, complete with formal pools and statuary. Conversely, a naturalistic meadow would appear equally out of place surrounding a stately brick Tudor home. We all borrow from other places and other times when conceiving our garden visions. Translating them into reality is what it's all about. For example, my garden is a hybrid between the classic perennial border garden and a cottage garden. Some might claim, "You can't do an English garden in Denver!" (or Kansas City or Charlotte or wherever you live). But they've disregarded the fact that any style of garden is simply that—a style. Had I planted mine with plants that thrive in England, I'd be doomed to failure. As it is, my English-themed garden has a Colorado twist, featuring flowers that survive and thrive in my dry, hot-in-summer, cold-in-winter climate. Plants don't know or care about style; they're satisfied when they get the right spot in the right garden.

■ Garden Rooms

Rooms organize a house. Most of us bathe in one room, cook in another, sleep, do laundry, play, read, and watch TV in others. Some rooms do double duty. Others don't do much. Unlike its namesake, for instance, the living room is often the least lived-in room in the house.

Rooms can also organize a garden (and they are really "living" rooms), even if they're not strictly for daily activities. When I'm in the garden, I'd just as soon ignore dirty dishes, piles of laundry, and the day's top stories. Time spent in a garden is unlike any other activity. Some days it's all about color and excitement. Others are about manicuring and attention to details. War is occasionally declared on weeds, while every once in awhile a day is dreamy and peaceful.

My garden is organized into several rooms. Some are for the pleasure and convenience of people, others for the specific requirements of the plants in them (shade, sun, moisture, etc.). As with the rooms of a house, these garden rooms demand care and attention. Like an interior designer who creates a room, I rarely get to use it the way it's intended. I'm more of a maid with dirty nails and knees. But that's my own fault: I've made my (garden) bed, now I must lie in it.

When friends come over, I'm forced to enjoy my garden. While I join in the conversation, music, and wine, however, I'm secretly thinking that the flowering maple over there is looking droopy and I've just got to get those bug-bitten leaves off the golden sweet potato vine. And that begonia really ought to be deadheaded. Right now! Pretty gardens do require time and the right kind of work at the right time. But perhaps the emphasis I've placed on the work involved to create one is misleading. It's not really work, after all, if it's something you enjoy. A garden is much more than a place in which to work. It's a place to live.

PLANNING A GARDEN ROOM

Let's focus on creating a garden room for a well-balanced, moderately industrious gardener. What do you plan to do in your garden room? In a conventional house, the activities are already assigned by room before we even move in. Their size, shape, fixtures, and location already determine how they're to be used. A stove or a tub is a good indicator. The rooms without appliances give us a little more wiggle room to turn them into something besides a spare bedroom, such as a library, sewing room, or home theater.

A garden room starts from scratch. At the start, the only thing that it has in common with an indoor room is a floor. In most cases, it has no walls, windows, ceilings, furniture, or ornaments. Sometimes, such as in the city, walls of other buildings define the garden space. New

**A former concrete patio slab has been transformed into a peaceful room—perfect for knitting—
with the addition of brick pavers, comfy wicker, and pots of blue lily-of-the-Nile.**

Yorkers know all about this. But many people simply have a "yard," which is usually the lawn, trees, and shrubs that surround the house. The closest most yards get to having a room is the patio, oftentimes a concrete afterthought tacked onto the back of the house.

A real garden room can serve as an extension of the home. Your lifestyle will help you decide how it should be designed, whether for dining, entertaining, catnapping, or all of the above. Creating one room leads to another. Any garden appears larger when it's segmented and all is not apparent at first glance. Other garden rooms can be simply for display, showcasing a collection of plants the way we display trophies, books, and figurines inside. Taking the concept of a room too literally, collectors sometimes find a way to clutter it up with non-plant items. Take the case of an elderly couple I once saw on British TV who collected more than 500 gnomes. The broadcast showed them demolishing their collection with sledgehammers. When asked why, the lady of the house replied, "It got to be a bit much, really." I'm sure there's a lesson for all of us in this.

Getting back to the business of creating a room, the only thing that is absolutely necessary is a sense of enclosure. This can start perhaps with a wall or walls of a building and include fences, pillars, planters, and screens as well as living elements such as hedges and potted plants. Most of us don't like to sit in a room without windows (except at the movies) so the enclosure doesn't need to be thorough. A garden room doesn't necessarily need a ceiling, but it becomes more intimate with some sort of canopy, whether it's a tree, arbor, pergola, or even an umbrella.

> I'd rather dine in a garden than in the fanciest restaurant in the world.

DINING IN THE GARDEN

When I picture creating a garden room, I think about food. I'd rather dine in a garden than in the fanciest restaurant in the world. For one thing, I'm already dressed for it. For another, a summer's evening breeze scented by lilies or angel's trumpets enhances any meal (even one I cook). But even great tastes and scents are secondary if you're uncomfortable, so consider what you and your guests will sit on for a meal in an outdoor dining room. Teak, wrought iron, and cast aluminum—they're all great choices, depending on your taste. I don't go in for plastic—it just doesn't fit in with any of my garden concepts—but because this type of furniture is inexpensive, you can use it initially until you can find and afford what you really like. Furniture makes a design statement in a garden dining room. Sometimes it says, "French café," "English tea time," "Southern elegance," or "Laguna Beach lunch." I'm not exactly sure what mine says except maybe, "This looks comfy," mainly due to cushions and pillows. I'm constantly shuttling them inside when rain clouds appear, but they help to set a mood.

Mood is what a garden room is all about. You create it. It's a room like no other, always changing. And what's even better, a little dirt is perfectly acceptable. Some of my favorite moments have been spent in my outdoor dining room, never mind my compulsive gardening and inability to relax. I recall chili on a cold day, a cool salad on a warm night, the excitement of planting containers each spring, and just hanging out with my pets. I love watching the cats stalk butterflies and the dogs snoozing under the table or "helping" me with watering and deadheading.

A garden room isn't just about entertaining and relaxing. I don't relax much in the vegetable and herb room. I sweat. There's a chair and table in the shade to take a break, but the focus here is production. Though some people integrate vegetables and herbs into the rest of the garden, many gardeners like a separate area dedicated to them. Or they put vegetables and flowers for cutting together (a cutting garden). Some of us just find it too difficult to pick from the garden for fear it would spoil the show. I'm reluctant to pick from my main borders, too.

■ Beds and Borders

Let's talk about beds and borders. What's the difference? There really isn't much. A bed is usually a flat patch of ground, often carved out of the lawn. Traditionally, it displays bright

Where no rules apply, annuals, perennials, and shrubs stuff beds (or are they borders?) carved informally from the lawn. The plantings include roses, lupines, black-eyed Susans, penstemons, and dianthus.

summer annuals, such as petunias and geraniums, commonly known as "bedding" plants. At one time, when Britannia ruled the waves and Queen Victoria sat on the throne of England, bedding was all the rage. You could show off your wealth based on how grand, intricate, and labor-intensive your garden beds were. We don't see much of this in home gardens any longer, but remnants of it linger in municipal parks every summer. Occasionally a town or city will spell out its name in marigolds, for example. A local hotel tried this a couple of years ago using petunias. It was fairly legible as you drove by in early summer, but as the petunias grew and spread, the hotel name became a blur. The Victorians had enormous gardening staffs to snip and clip. At any rate, we don't bed so much these days.

By contrast, we make borders. A border is largely a European concept, especially English, which replaces beds of annuals with beds of perennials. We'll talk about these kinds of plants in detail later in the book, but suffice it to say that perennials live for many years and come up "perennially" each year, while annuals usually live up to their name and must be planted anew each year. By the very word "border," you might imagine that this piece of ground borders something, such as a wall, walkway, or property line. It can, of course, border something, but it's come to mean an arrangement of perennials usually in long, rectangular expanses. My "borders" are really just two equal strips of earth about 60' by 10' with a path down the middle. Some people like lawns running down their borders or a layer of fine pea gravel that crunches as you walk. A border can run alongside a driveway or fence, go uphill if it has to, and it doesn't even have to be straight. Borders traditionally have some sort of backing to them such as a wall or hedge. A lot of the English ones employ romantically crumbling brick walls. Mine has a picket fence. Whatever it is, the backing serves as a sort of device like a picture frame to set off the beauty of the plants.

Though a border used to be strictly about perennials, it's come to include just about every kind of plant you'd like to toss in it. This "mixed border" concept is a boon to kitchen-sink gardeners like me who wish to incorporate roses, tulips, basil, and anything else we fancy.

> Most of us are essentially cottage gardeners when we start, and after years of experimentation—becoming increasingly sophisticated—we often return to our cottage roots.

The most important part about a border is its complete lack of regimentation. This means no rows and essentially no strict rules. A beautiful border does, however, need a bit of discipline both in its planning and maintenance to keep from looking chaotic. For that we'll discuss colors, shapes, textures, and the sequence of blooms—later.

You've probably heard about "cottage gardens" as much as borders. They're planted just about the same as borders, really, but I'd say that they're especially exuberant and expressive. A famous British garden writer once called cottage gardens "undisciplined masses of flopping vegetation." When they became all the rage, he wrote a glowing book about them. Most of us are essentially cottage gardeners when we start, and after years of experimentation—becoming increasingly sophisticated—we often return to our cottage roots. I used to care far more about clever combinations. Last summer, I accidentally grew a blood red dahlia in a pot with magenta petunias, chartreuse sweet potato vine, and orange cigar plant. It was absolutely hideous and I didn't give a hoot. I'm definitely back to my exuberant cottage phase.

■ Rocks in the Garden

Rock gardeners are just cottage gardeners with rocks. They specialize in smaller plants, often from mountainous areas, that grow best amongst rocks, especially in the crevices. Rock gardeners almost always display meticulous grooming techniques as well as a huge thirst to try new plants. Gardening with rocks is a bit different than pure rock gardening. Many people garden with natural rock formations on their properties. Others haul in rocks to pay homage to the natural landscape of their regions.

My sister and I did this—in our own ways—when we were kids. On family trips to the mountains, we were allowed to bring home rocks we collected. Betty and I managed some fairly large-sized rocks that we put in the back of our family station wagon. We saved those for our rock gardens, which we planted with creeping phlox and hen and chicks and populated with

**Stone, wood, and water characterize a Japanese-inspired garden,
with breathtaking water lilies inviting reflection.**

our pet turtles. My sister and I built rock gardens all over the place. It's great to have gardening parents who don't worry about what the neighbors think of their children's latest creation.

Japanese and Chinese styles of gardens often employ rocks in their designs, but for entirely different reasons than creating plant habitats. Many gardeners enjoy bringing Asian elements into their home gardens, as well as evoking the styles of planting. Stone, wood, and water can be used in many ways to evoke an Asian look. One word of caution: the architecture of your home must lend itself to these styles. Simplicity of line and ornament is critical to do justice to your interpretation of a Japanese garden surrounding your home. My understanding is that Japanese gardens, in particular, serve as artistic microcosms of the natural world. Before you do a sand garden or throw up a teahouse, investigate this discipline of gardening thoroughly. As with European styles of gardening, use plants suitable to your region in an Asian-inspired garden.

■ Naturalistic Gardens

Wherever you live, you'll find gardens that mirror the natural landscape. One of the strongest garden movements today is about prairies, plains, and meadows. There aren't many left of the virgin grasslands that used to cover so much of this continent. Cornfields and pastures have largely supplanted the plains. I have a particular appreciation for the plants I grew up with on the plains. From the edge of town where we lived, an endless sea of grasses stretched to the horizon.

Prairie and meadow gardens strive to present the beauty of these habitats. Besides the predominant grasses, these gardens also feature many of the wildflowers that, because of their toughness and beauty, have become garden stalwarts throughout the world, such as Indian blanket, goldenrod, aster, gayfeather, and coreopsis.

Most flowers were once wild, except for those "bred in captivity." Through breeding and selection, plants from around the world have blossomed into the ones that we grow in our gardens today. Hybrid tea roses, for example, aren't to be found just growing down by the side of the ditch. As "wild" subjects, many forerunners of modern hybrids look quite different. Modern dahlias, zinnias, and marigolds (all native to Mexico) have become big, bold, and brassy in comparison to the original wild plants. For many gardeners, the charm of the originals far outweighs the "improvements" by breeders.

These are what we usually think of when we picture wildflowers. They vary from region to region, of course, with some having a very large range and others being quite localized. Many

A rustic fence is all that separates these "captive" columbines from the untamed woods beyond; seedlings will likely jump the fence in the coming years.

> **I've never met a fresh vegetable I didn't like, and that includes Brussels sprouts, squash, and even okra.**

gardeners enjoy going "native," planting and growing the wild species of their regions. Already adapted to your soil and climate, they will probably prove to be tough and enduring.

■ Garden Edibles

Despite the fact that this introduction to gardening does not focus on edible plants, I wanted to be sure to offer a few tips to those of you who will not be content with a strictly ornamental garden. Growing up in a gardening family gave me an appreciation for working in the soil, even at a very early age, and for more than just growing plants. I also liked hoeing rows, planting seeds, and especially harvesting. Kids are notoriously fussy about eating vegetables (and often turn into fussy adults). But children in gardening families never need to be prodded to eat their peas, beets, or beans.

I've never met a fresh vegetable I didn't like, and that includes Brussels sprouts, squash, and even okra. I salivate just writing about homegrown corn and tomatoes. The popularity of farmer's markets testifies to our appreciation of freshly picked vegetables. As soon as a vegetable is picked, its sugar begins to turn to starch and the flavor fades. Carrots, corn, and peas are decidedly more delicious if eaten straight from the garden (or, in my case, in the garden; peas rarely make it to the kitchen).

Taste isn't the only reason to raise your own vegetables. With the tremendous popularity of pesticide-free, organically grown produce, it makes sense to raise your own healthy crops. The key is not to panic at the arrival of the first aphid. You can manage outbreaks of pests using soap. That's right, soap. Pure garden soap that you mix with water is available at garden centers. It doesn't poison insects, but instead dissolves their hard exoskeletons. Like the Wicked Witch of the West, they melt away. Explain that to your kids and they'll be thrilled to help spray the soap.

While pests are always a cause of concern, the most important aspect of growing vegetables is your soil. Although a loose, friable (crumbly) soil is ideal, a lack of it doesn't mean you're out of luck. Homeowners with heavy clay soil and high-rise dwellers without any soil at all have options. Raised beds filled with fertile topsoil can be created, and heavy soils can be improved by incorporating organic matter. And almost anybody with a balcony that receives at least a half-day's sun can grow vegetables in containers.

Root crops such as beets, turnips, carrots, onions, and radishes grow best in very loose soil with the consistency of store-bought potting soil. They have a difficult time extending their roots into heavy or rocky soil. Raised beds and large containers provide that ideal, loose growing medium.

As you plan your vegetable garden, choose a spot that receives plenty of sun. Some people don't consider a vegetable garden very pretty and hide it behind the garage or along the alley. Don't fall into that trap. Find the best spot for growing vegetables and turn it into a beautiful space. It can hold its own as a viable garden room if you enclose it with nice fencing or hedges, dress it up with ornaments such as a birdbath (birds should always be welcome to dine on insects), and create an interesting layout with paths and paving. Trellises and arbors add further architectural interest and support climbers such as pole beans, peas, and squash. Many gardeners add flowers to their vegetable garden, especially edible ones such as pansies, nasturtiums, and sweet Williams.

Vegetables are split into two groups: cool-season and warm-season. At the beginning of the growing season (cool season), depending on where you live, you can plant seeds or transplant young nursery seedlings of lettuce, spinach, peas, beets, radishes, and onions. They can withstand a light frost—even snow—and develop rapidly during cool, sunny weather. When the real heat hits (warm season), spinach and lettuce will bolt (send up flowering stalks), and their usefulness is over. Radishes become bitter and woody and peas cease flowering and become magnets for spider mites. Pull up these cool-season plants and compost them, and plant heat-loving vegetables in their place. Warm soil is essential for beans, corn, and squash to germinate well.

More tomatoes succumb to bad judgment about timing than any other crop. Peppers are right up there, too. Don't jump the gun: One unseasonably hot day doesn't mean it's safe to plant your warm-season crops. Tomatoes and peppers grow so quickly that even those planted in early June in northern gardens and in mountainous areas will rapidly catch up and soon surpass plants set out too early. Neither can stand one degree below freezing, and cool nights will stunt their growth for the entire season. Pay attention to the night temperatures in your area—they must stay reliably above 50 degrees; daily highs are irrelevant.

My best tip for growing great tomatoes (the favorite of most gardeners) is to bury a young transplant all the way up to its set of lower leaves. Tomatoes root all along the stem this way, ensuring a sturdy, well-rooted plant. Keep the soil evenly moist, feed regularly with a fertilizer formulated especially for tomatoes, and pick and stomp pesky tomato hornworms. Nothing beats the taste of a homegrown tomato. Each bite is memorable. I can almost taste it now.

■ Container Gardening

For everything you want to grow but don't think you can, there's container gardening. You control the soil, fertilizer, and water to accommodate most any plant you've been hankering to grow. The 300 pots on my patio and balcony are a testament to a lot of hankering.

Start with large pots of at least 10" or 12" diameters. Any smaller and you'll never be able to keep the soil within them moist (my small pots get good use housing my collection of succulents and cactus, which don't need much water). Terra-cotta pots "breathe," meaning that their porous walls allow both air and moisture to penetrate the walls. While that's beneficial to roots, it's not so good if the pots dry out on a hot day when you're not home. Containers made of fiberglass, wood, plastic, and glazed pottery don't breathe and consequently hold moisture better. Use potting soil (bags of commercially available soil labeled "potting soil" can be found at any nursery or garden supply store); garden soil rarely makes a suitable growing medium in pots.

You can create beautiful combinations of plants by blending upright, rounded, and trailing plants for a balanced effect. Plant them very tightly together for a lush look right off the bat. Fertilize every week to ten days to get great "magazine cover" results. Some plants may be best grown as single specimens in their own pots. They can then be grouped with other pots. I use bricks, blocks, and overturned pots beneath my

> With container gardening you control the soil, fertilizer, and water to accommodate most any plant you've been hankering to grow.

A low stone wall elevates pots of flowers for an up-close experience, including oxalis, pink spider lily, pale pink Asiatic lilies, magenta stock, and white alstroemeria.

containers to stage them for the best show. I try to get many of them up to eye level so I can enjoy them when I'm dining or writing. Conversely, lower your hanging baskets so you're not just staring at the bottom of the basket.

Individual pots or groupings of them serve as focal points in the garden, disguise eyesores, direct traffic flow, provide screening, and mainly beautify our outdoor living spaces. Though we think of container plantings essentially for summer color, they're useful anytime, not only in frost-free climates but in cold ones as well. Holly, evergreens, and ornamental grasses can be especially attractive with a light dusting of snow. Also, containers can host dwarf fruit trees, evergreens, flowering shrubs, bulbs, and almost everything else that is ordinarily grown in the ground. (Rooftop and balcony gardeners need big pots and planters for some of these options.)

■ Watery Effects

A pond, reflecting pool, or fountain serves as cooling relief from summer's heat and glare. Gardeners' ponds play a vital role for birds, both for drinking and bathing. Even if you have no intention of ever installing a water feature in your garden, at least provide a bowl of clean water. The birds will revel in it and repay you by eating your unwanted insects.

When you do take the plunge and become a water gardener, you'll enter an exciting new world with its own lingo. Soon, you'll talk liners, pumps, filters, fish, and algae like a pro. You'll fall in love with water lilies and my favorite, the lotus. With its graceful blue-green leaves and elegant pink flowers, it's no wonder the lotus was used by ancient Egyptians as a recurring artistic motif.

Beyond water lilies and lotus, a pond may host many beautiful aquatics, especially those plants that thrive at water's edge. Some are hardy and may be planted directly in the mucky soil where their roots stay perpetually wet, while others are kept in their pots and submerged below water level. Among the loveliest of these plants are Japanese and Louisiana irises as well as *Iris pseudacorus*, the fabled yellow fleur-de-lis of France. Rushes, reeds, and cattails are also perfect for the water's edge, along with tropical elephant ears (*Colocasia*), pickerel, papyrus, and water cannas. The dramatic foliage of rodgersias and ligularias can be stunning, topped by pink or golden flowers, respectively. Some water plants simply float. Water hyacinth, water lettuce, and duckweed migrate around the pond with the breeze. The first two should only be allowed in enclosed ponds, as they have become major pests in the South, escaping into and clogging waterways.

Deciding what sort of water feature you want is the most important part. It takes a deft touch to pull off a naturalistic pond. Unless you have a lot of space (in full sun, by the way), it's difficult to make your pond convincing. How many of us city dwellers have a natural spring and a rock outcropping in our backyards? In the country or where there are hills and rock formations, the illusion is far more convincing, but a more formal approach may work best for most of us.

A convincingly naturalistic pond teems with life such as an orange canna, rushes, water lilies, and golden yellow ligularia.

My raised pond, about 4' by 8', doesn't pretend to be natural. It has provided me with hours of entertainment as well as some strange encounters. You may meet some big birds. Herons may come for a tasty meal. A light on your pond at night is the equivalent of the famed golden arches to night-flying herons. Some water gardeners resort to netting over their ponds, but the best idea comes from my friends Susan and Rhonda, who bought black plastic boxes (about the size of a bread box) at a home improvement store. The boxes, intended for some sort of plumbing, have holes for tubes and pipes so the fish can swim in and out and hide inside. It works like a charm.

Raccoons regularly mug my pond. Whether it's to wash or eat (there always seem to be fewer fish after one of their visits), they just trash my pond. I put mousetraps on the pond's edge to deter them. The fish population seems to rebound from the predations and only once have I needed to start from scratch. Several winters ago, a warm day lured my goldfish to the surface. The temperature plunged suddenly, trapping them in the ice. This is known as the "great fish stick episode." The adventure continues.

■ Color Basics

We've talked plenty about plants, although barely mentioning what draws us to them: color. We're all so different. And we see color differently. Some of us are cautious or confused about color. Others, like me, tend to collect one or two kinds of plants and give scant thought to color combinations. Then there are the magpies, who are attracted to bright, shiny objects, and have one of everything. There are also the minimalists, whose color palette is extremely limited. And finally, there are those with a "survival garden," where the color scheme is based on what hasn't died.

Unfortunately, too many of us never find out what we really like because we're scared to experiment. Whether it's our home, wardrobe, or garden, we're so unsure and afraid of making mistakes that we limit ourselves before we even start. Many people stick with the equivalent of a black cocktail dress. They play it safe.

Comparing colors of apparel and garden flowers isn't quite fair, but I think people confuse them. You have no idea how many times I've heard a client say, "I hate orange," or "I loathe yellow." It's too bad that somewhere between our first box of crayons and adulthood we learned to hate a particular color. I have to respect this prejudice, of course, but on what is it based? If it's because you look hideous in yellow or orange, don't wear it. Clothing is next to our skin and hair; flowers bloom against a green background.

> To begin experimenting with color, take one base color and repeat it over and over in your plantings.

Coats of color paint the garden throughout the season. Planning helps to match them with the appropriate time. Our psychological needs should be considered in the process. In northern states, for example, gardeners are hungry—no, ravenous—for spring color after a monochromatic winter. In summer, blues and lavenders provide a slight respite from the heat. And in fall, gold and orange match our moods, even if they might seem out of sync at any other time. There's no reason to exclude any color from the garden; just find the season where it best fits.

The palette of spring plantings can be among the weirdest. Maybe it's because the fall-planted bulbs aren't ever compared with the perennials with which they'll bloom until they erupt into a big spring clash. After all, a tulip is just a picture on a bag when we plant it. Small wonder that some combinations are excessively cheerful. Red tulips and basket-of-gold are the visual equivalents of nails on a chalkboard to me. Yellow daffodils and hot pink creeping phlox I find equally disturbing. I actually like this perennial and employ it frequently, especially soft pink 'Candy Stripe' and 'Emerald Blue', although the latter is so deceivingly named. Its color is delicate lavender-blue. (The color peacemakers in the garden are blue, purple, or lavender.) I've usually found that almost all pastels go together without much trouble and that all intense colors—let's call them jewel tones—work well together.

Because color can be so personal and so emotional, I don't believe in assigning rules about it. Even if I did, I also believe that rules are for breaking. There are some tips, however,

Pretty in pink, these Asiatic lilies, pincushion flowers, and rose campion get a boost from the chartreuse leaves of variegated yucca and golden hops vine.

that can help a bit when approaching color. To begin experimenting with color, take one base color and repeat it over and over in your plantings. This is similar to painting the walls of a room with a consistent color. Since we were discussing lavender-blue anyway, consider how soothing it is and how many perennials and shrubs feature lavender-blue flowers, from veronicas and catmints to salvias and butterfly bushes. This color can span the seasons, providing a base for adding bolder jewel tones.

The same base color could be pink, yellow, or white. Then you can go off in any direction that suits you and the season. In the case of lavender-blue, add some deeper blues and purples and you've set the stage for hot pink or coral accents, or perhaps even orange. Oddly enough, if you take the base colors of pink, yellow, or white and add darker blues and purples, you've set up exactly the same situation. A base color plus purple is the ideal way to incorporate jewel tones into the garden, whether they're golden California poppies, ruby roses, magenta wine cups (*Callirhoe involucrata*), or orange tiger lilies.

The base color idea is also practical for those who collect plants that span a wide color range, such as irises or lilies. Sometimes these flowers come in unusual shades—or several at one time—that are a bit hard to fit in gracefully. A simple base color background pulls it all together. For the magpie gardeners, who are attracted to bright colors and pick up one of this and one of that until their gardens look like button collections, add a base color to make some semblance of order out of the hodgepodge. This could be as simple as broadcasting (i.e., spreading) a half pound of bachelor's buttons or sweet alyssum seeds (in a single color, not a mix) to fill in the gaps and provide unity.

Minimalist schemes are often great experiments—in the beginning. If you create a garden room that's limited in color (and you become as tired of it as I became of my all-white border), try adding the equivalent of throw pillows. Toss in one new color each season—even if it's just a foliage contrast—such as lime green in an all-yellow garden or burgundy in all-pink or -red one.

Finally—and you know who you are—there are those with a color scheme based on what's left from what you planted last year. Plenty of gardens start out with lovely color schemes, but the voles ate the tulips, the daisies croaked last winter, and the astilbe succumbed during the drought. What's left doesn't hang together. I've seen living rooms like this too. The walls used to match the sofa that the cat shredded, and the new chintz chairs were such a great deal, even though they're not that great with the plaid upholstery on the new sofa.

Let's make it simple. Pick one accent foliage color, such as silver, and three colors (make one of them bright) say pale pink, powder blue, and magenta. If you've already planted, dig out everything that doesn't fit this scheme and give these strays to your neighbors. Go to the nursery. Splurge.

■ Think Ahead When Buying

Keep in mind that summer and fall flowers are not in bloom in spring; two-thirds of your purchases should be for coming seasons. Spring may seem like an odd time to plan for fall color in the garden, but each autumn we do the reverse, planting crocuses, daffodils, and tulips to greet us in spring. It makes sense to take advantage of our early-season enthusiasm to ensure a colorful garden late in the year.

Summer heat often puts a damper on planting. If it's hot and/or dry, it's both tiring and risky to plant perennials. And let's face it: We buy what's in bloom. Most people purchase their plants in spring. Blooming annuals and perennials fly off the garden center shelves. The gallon pots of later-blooming perennials, devoid of bloom, get passed by. If you truly want a profusion of bloom throughout the season, a full half of your spring purchases should be strictly green. That's right, no flowers. To do this, you need to do some homework. What late bloomers are suitable for your garden?

People who need instant gratification will need to steel themselves. It's difficult to resist color. If you buy smart, your garden will be as beautiful in September as in June, if not more so. Don't forget the crescendo effect: by combining annuals with late-blooming perennials, the color will intensify throughout the summer and into fall. Many annuals reach their peaks in late August and September, coinciding with the explosion of fall-blooming perennials. Annual zinnias, dahlias, gomphrenas, verbenas, sweet potato vines, and black-eyed Susans hit their stride just as perennial asters, mums, hummingbird trumpets, plumbagos, coneflowers, Japanese anemones, and ornamental grasses come into their own.

Planting late bloomers in spring gives them almost an entire season to grow and perform. Even small-sized plants, with proper care, can put on a great show, although they'll be even more amazing in coming years. There's an old saying about perennials: "The first year they sleep, the second year they creep, the third year they leap." They may leap a little faster than the old adage—depending on the attention and fertilizer you lavish upon them—but have patience for a year or two.

■ Weed Strategies

Dreams do come true in fairy tales (and sometimes in gardens), but it's usually after plenty of toil and suffering. In fairy tales, the usual cause of all the turmoil is the wicked stepmother. In gardens, it's the weeds. During the excitement of planning and planting, weeds aren't on our minds. We're dreaming of tulips and roses and tomatoes. How dare weeds give us a wake-up call?!

Everyone wants a magic "cure" for weeds. For the kind of garden I like and design, there isn't one. I don't use or recommend black plastic, landscape fabric, weed barrier cloth, or smothering bark nuggets. They're just not natural. The only way to achieve a real garden is with real sweat. And that means weeding.

Weeds are a fact of life. Whenever we turn a spadeful of earth, we're exposing opportunistic seeds. Developing a strategy for coping with them is part of making a new garden or enlarging an existing one. In one category are the really bad, horrible weeds. Whoever said that a weed is just a flower growing in the wrong spot must have been on heavy medication or never ran into the likes of bindweed, kudzu, bittersweet, thistle, and various ivies. You probably know about the worst thugs in your neighborhood. They're basically despised for their aggression, tenacity, and deep roots. In the other category are the pesky weeds, slightly less aggravating because of their annual nature. These include portulaca, wild lettuce, shepherd's purse, mare's tail, lamb's quarters, hen bit, dandelion, pigweed, and knotweed. It's funny that so many carry picturesque—even cute—common names. Their greatest strength is in their numbers—kajillions of them.

I've never had the good fortune to start one of my own gardens on a piece of property that didn't host a couple of really bad thugs. Sometimes they've even fooled me into thinking I'd conquered them, only to discover they were just waiting until I'd planted before rearing their ugly heads again. My best piece of advice is to make sure they're good and dead before you plant. The method of killing them is up to you and depends on the nature of the villains.

The worst possible thing to do is to rototill if you're facing a persistent, deep-rooted weed such as bindweed. For a week or so, you'll pat yourself on the back. But soon every piece you chopped up will become a new weed. The best control for these sorts of weeds might be to use an herbicide or to smother them with a layer of plastic or newspapers for up to a year. My personal method is to pull them over and over—up to six times—to weaken the plant, then to hit them with an herbicide such as Round-up. My rampaging crop of bindweed appears to be (nearly) extinct, but the tree of heaven that came with

> Whoever said that a weed is just a flower growing in the wrong spot must have been on heavy medication or never ran into the likes of bindweed, kudzu, bittersweet, thistle, and various ivies.

the place sends out runners as effortlessly as most of us send e-mails. There's even one growing in my laundry room. Yes, in it. I've chopped, dug, and sprayed, but it's a battle of wills. Ordinarily I wouldn't credit a tree with the ability to form intent, but I do wonder when it mounts a home invasion.

When you've conquered the really tough weeds (or if you lucked out and never had to face them at all), the first-year garden still offers challenges. Weeding can take the fun out of the whole experience. It seems never-ending, as weeds of different kinds take their turns and germinate throughout the growing season. Many weed seeds can lie dormant for years or decades, just waiting for an opportunity.

My most persistent of the pesky weeds last season in a new garden area was portulaca. Springing up as thick as dog hair, this fleshy-leafed annual thrives in hot, dry weather, much like its ornamental cousin we usually call moss rose. There was nothing rosy about this picture. Whereas most annuals that I hoe or pluck have the decency to die, portulaca often re-roots. I like to use a tool called an "action" or "shuffle" hoe for annual weeds. It looks a bit like a horseshoe mounted on a handle, with a flat, two-sided blade that cuts just beneath the crust of the soil as you rake it back and forth. It's very useful, but I go back with a rake to pick up the portulaca before it roots again.

I went through about five rounds with the portulaca, cleaning out every last one before a new batch would sprout a week or so later. Cooler temperatures finally turned the tide in my favor, so I expect very little resistance this coming season. The perennials will begin to expand, shading much of the ground, leaving less and less opportunity for portulaca or any other weeds. The third year in a garden for me is generally almost weed-free, leaving more time for the more rewarding chores.

Weeding does have its good points, depending on how efficient you become. There are days I actually enjoy it. Good tools help. A really sturdy dandelion digger is perfect for tap-rooted weeds. Don't buy a cheap one; it won't last a week without bending. I rely heavily on my Japanese fisherman's knife, often called a hori-hori. It can serve for tap-rooted weeds as well as shallow-rooted weeds, because the edge is serrated to cut just below the soil surface. Several kinds of hoes are useful as well, from the previously mentioned hollow type to the standard flat blade or smaller dagger-pointed variety for tight spaces. And some people prefer their bare hands, wrestling victory from the earth in hand-to-hand combat.

Weeding takes up valuable time, so we need to make the most of it. I often play music on headphones. Sometimes I sing. My neighbors frown on this. During the attack of the portulaca, I used the reward system on myself. It goes something like this: "If I get as far as that butterfly bush (or whatever landmark selected), I'll stop for a while, sit in the shade, and possibly find the strength to go inside and find some chocolate." The weeds are gone and I'm still using this system. Now that's a happy ending.

■ Insects, Pests, and Diseases in the Garden

My parents never used insecticides in their garden, so I've grown up pretty ignorant of them. And I intend to keep it that way. People freak out at the sight of the first aphid of the year and overreact with an arsenal of chemical weapons. My advice? Chill. A bug-free garden is as unnatural as one made of artificial flowers. As I've mentioned before, soap is a gardener's best friend. I mix a teaspoon of Dr. Bronner's Castille Oil soap in a spray bottle with a quart of water and have at it. Spraying any pesky aphids I can see (you've got to hit them for the soap to dissolve them), I also make sure to hit the undersides of leaves and stems. This is where most sucking insects like aphids, spider mites, and white flies hang out.

Then there are the chewing insects like caterpillars, beetles, and earwigs. I hate earwigs. It's not that they do any more damage than any other bug; it's just that they're furtive like cockroaches with little pincers in front. I've seen enough science fiction movies to be totally creeped out by the threat they could pose to all humanity.

For every bad bug in the garden, there's one on your side. And along with the ladybugs, lacewings, predatory wasps, praying mantis, and spiders (the good guys) is the bird and bat brigade, which feasts on insects. Start to tinker with this coalition by introducing poisons, and you'll destroy the natural balance. Would you begrudge the caterpillars a meal or two before they transform into butterflies? And no matter how careful you are with chemical sprays and dusts, do you really want to take chances with children, pets, fish, and wildlife?

Of course, there may be critters that you would like to banish from your garden. Depending on where you live, perhaps you'll tangle with mice, squirrels, voles, moles, ground squirrels, gophers, rabbits, skunks, raccoons, deer, elk, or moose—or some combination thereof. Consult your local experts at botanical gardens, nurseries, and extension services on how best to deal with whatever is plaguing you. There are some truly destructive insects and critters out there with which I've never had to deal. Perhaps you may need to at some point. All I can say is that I'd urge you to take the most conservative approach. It never hurts to consult the seasoned gardeners in your neighborhood. Odds are, they've seen it all and may have some clever, environmentally friendly remedies. Approaches work differently in some regions and at certain times of the year.

Some of your staunchest allies are your pets. Both cats and dogs can be deterrents to wildlife, whether they're aggressive protectors or just hanging out on the porch. The mere scent of dogs, for example, puts off deer. I met a man in Montana with a beautiful garden out in the country that wasn't fenced (usually the only reliable way to keep deer out). He'd trained his dog since he was a puppy to mark certain trees and rocks that ringed the property. He and the puppy walked and peed several times a day for several months until it became part of the dog's daily routine.

Still, I'd recommend fencing for best results, since deer will eat the shingles off your house if they're hungry enough. Much is made of deer-resistant plants that they will find unpalatable, as well as soap sprays, hot pepper sprays, blood meal, sirens, flashing lights, and heavy metal music. I'd imagine you'd mostly alarm your neighbors rather than have a lasting effect on a herd of deer with appetites bigger than those of teenagers. I think deer are beautiful creatures when I see them in the mountains, but I can't imagine them grazing in my garden. I think they'd quickly lose their charm. So put up some substantial fencing or get a puppy and go for a stroll.

Plant diseases are no fun. Some are not usually life-threatening, such as mildew, although others such as clematis wilt are fatal. Can you prevent most diseases? Not really. Can you avoid the plants that get them? You bet. Nursing sick plants is grim and depressing. A garden full of mildewed, black-spotted plants is common, but unnecessary. In any region there are hundreds, no thousands, of plants that stay healthy no matter how humid and muggy it gets. Some books will recommend "good air circulation," as if you could place giant fans in pertinent spots in your garden. When plants succumb to disease, they're most likely ill-suited to growing in your region. You can become nursemaid rather than gardener or decide that no matter how lovely a plant might be (somewhere else) you can find a new love. And it's always worth investigating varieties that have natural resistance or have been bred to be resistant.

■ Realistic Maintenance

How much work your garden requires depends on its size, complexity, and the types of plants you grow. It also depends on your temperament. Some of us can easily overlook flaws. Others have this compulsive need to be on top of everything all the time, so we're constantly snipping and clipping. And timing is everything.

When I was five years old, my family moved to a small town on the eastern plains of Colorado. Gardening was a hard-fought battle on that windswept land. My early memories are of flowers, from the lilac and bridal veil bushes that hugged our house, to tulips and tomatoes in the garden, to wild roses and asters in the fields next to our house.

I've gardened for more decades than I care to admit, and it's still a sweaty and dirty business; but I no longer think in terms of war. Fighting nature is an exercise in futility. Accepting soil and weather conditions—and welcoming challenges—yields the most rewards. Knowing what to do—and when—makes gardening a pleasure rather than a chore (depending, of course, on how you feel about sweat and dirt).

Each spring I observe great mistakes. Apartment dwellers imagine their houseplants would appreciate a little sunshine as much as they do and drag them to the balcony; ficus trees and ferns bake to a crisp. Blooming delphiniums and roses fresh from the greenhouse get planted in suburban gardens way too early; a late snowstorm inevitably flattens them like pancakes.

The trickiest time of the gardening season begins in midspring. The key is to balance enthusiasm with caution. Starved for color after our winter abstinence, some of us plant recklessly without consulting the calendar. Each region has a set date considered to be that of the average last frost. In my region, May 15 is the green light to set out warm-season favorites such as tomatoes, peppers, marigolds, and zinnias. But May 15 doesn't come with a guarantee, and it's actually too late for the cool-season annuals such as peas, spinach, leaf lettuce, and pansies. This will likely prove true in your region as well.

In truth, the gardening season begins much earlier than most people think and ends much later as well. Learning what gets planted when—and where—is vitally important. Novice gardeners try to buy tulip bulbs in spring, never guessing that their window of opportunity closed in late fall. Sun-loving roses languish beneath a canopy of trees, while shade-loving hostas fry in a sunny hot spot. Yankees who move down south stick to their old habits and plant their pansies just in time to roast them to a crisp. There's no need. We all make mistakes, and good gardeners learn from them. Just avoid the obvious ones. If you're not killing some plants from time to time, you're not trying very hard to learn how to garden. Experience, of course, is the best teacher. I still kill my fair share of plants; it's just more embarrassing for me.

Perhaps we should talk a bit about shopping before we talk about the art of planting and the other garden skills. Shopping is one of my favorite parts of gardening. You say you're good at it? You'll make a great gardener. Shop in stores throughout the season and from winter catalogs

Imagine the pleasure of tending this productive plot devoted to squash and corn, as well as to flowers for cutting—cosmos, marigolds, and sunflowers.

and your garden will never be dull. I rarely see crummy, poorly grown plants at a nursery these days, so I'm not going to go into a long spiel about selecting healthy plants. Look for good foliage color and you might check beneath the leaves for bugs—but I don't do that, so why should you? There will probably be a few roots poking out from the drainage holes in the bottom of the plant's pot. That's fine. If they're longer than a few inches and the root ball is threatening to bust out, the plant is known as "pot bound." This hasn't ever stopped me from buying a plant. You simply take it home, cut it out of its plastic prison, and try to trim and help separate the roots a bit. Then give it a loving home in the ground or a new pot.

■ Basic Skills

There are a few basic skills to learn to become a good gardener. They're all easily mastered. Most become second nature in time. Intuition plays a big part in figuring out what to do and

Whoever writes nursey tags for plants lives in a Camelot of gardening where plants reach amazing proportions never seen elsewhere.

when. Avoid making work for yourself. If everything looks all right, let sleeping dogs lie. Don't go out and hack at your bushes just because you think you should be doing something.

PLANTING

Planting is the most important skill you can learn. Do it gently, but firmly. The best way to learn is to watch an experienced gardener at work. Go to a botanical garden if there's one nearby to observe. Better yet, volunteer so you can get hands-on experience.

To plant your newly purchased plants, dig a hole larger than the pots in which they came. Turn the pots upside down with one hand, holding the other hand underneath to catch them, and coax the plants out gently (gravity will do most of the work); no yanking and pulling out by the stems. Plant them at the same level that they're growing in their pots, but in a slight depression. Gently pack the soil around the plant, but no stomping. Just use the strength in your hands.

As you work, build a little mud wall about 2" high around each plant to capture moisture. "Puddle in" each plant with a very slow trickle of the hose until it's thoroughly saturated. Each plant is essentially still in its container, so water deeply each time, probably every four to seven days for a gallon-size perennial, depending on your soil and weather. If you live in a cold winter area, fertilize every couple of weeks through July, and then stop so the plants can begin to prepare for cooler fall weather. In their second year, perennials need little or no fertilizer.

TRANSPLANTING

There comes a time when you'll want to divide and transplant a perennial. This is best done in early spring just as the plant emerges, but hardly anybody gets around to it then. You can basically do it any time except during the real summer heat. Dig it up (a digging fork is easiest, but a shovel will do). Cut it in half or in several pieces depending on its size. The blade of a spade works well. Give it a hard thrust. You can also use a sturdy kitchen knife.

Transplanting is just like planting, except that you usually give your subject a haircut before you replant. This generally means cutting back the top growth so the roots don't have so much to support while they're reestablishing themselves. The plant should end up at the same level it was growing at before you started. Again, create an earthen dam around the base to catch and hold water and thoroughly soak the soil immediately after planting.

GROWING FROM SEED

Sowing seeds is much less work than planting. Some kinds can be simply sprinkled over the soil as if you were feeding chickens. I usually do this in either fall or late winter with annuals such as larkspurs, poppies, and bachelor's buttons. Vegetable seeds are usually but not always planted in rows, at the appropriate time for each kind. After digging and leveling the site with a rake, use a hoe to create a furrow 1" or so deep. Then plant the corn, peas, beans, or whatever you like, covering the seeds about a ¼" to ½" deep. Space the seeds a few inches apart, knowing that as they germinate and grow, you'll need to thin them to allow room for each one to develop. How much to thin depends on what you're growing. Radishes need only a few inches in between, while corn needs a foot.

Sowing seeds inside is a bit easier, mainly because you're sitting down. The easiest way for most of us is to fill plastic six-pack plant containers with a soil mixture especially formulated for seedlings. Plant a few seeds per cell (you'll need to thin later), covering them as directed on the seed packet. Water from the bottom by soaking the containers in their trays or you'll probably wash the seeds all over the place. Seed packets also tell you when to plant, generally four to eight weeks before the average frost-free date in your area, so count backward from that date. It helps to get this all organized on paper in midwinter, plus it gives us something to dream about when winter seems never-ending.

SPACING PLANTS

How much room your plants need between them is very tricky. I pay attention to the growth estimates for trees and shrubs and space accordingly. For perennials and annuals, I tend to follow my own instincts because I don't trust the nursery tags. Whoever writes them lives in a far-off Camelot land of gardening where plants reach amazing proportions never seen elsewhere. So for where I live in the mountain West, I cut the recommended spacing down by at least a third and sometimes by half. My theory is that most of us prefer results during our lifetimes.

Glorious dahlias result from pinching, staking, fertilizing, and deadheading. They're worth the fuss.

FEEDING PLANTS

Once everything is planted and growing, feed your plants. There's no set standard; some plants are heavier feeders than others. Some don't want or need any supplemental fertilization at all. Just as a general guideline, be generous with roses, bulbs, most annuals, containerized plants, and vegetables. Most trees, shrubs, vines, herbs, and perennials can get along pretty well on their own. Many people overfeed their perennials and end up with a bunch of lax, floppy plants. Then they have to stake them. I don't like staking and I rarely grow plants that are bred to fall over, but occasionally I make an exception. You probably will, too.

PLANT SUPPORTS

My weakness is dahlias. The tall ones need stakes. I grow them in pots on my patio for their huge, eye-popping blossoms in the heat of summer and into fall. I pinch my dahlias when they're about 6" tall. This means I tweak out the growing tip with my thumb and forefinger. This causes them to branch out and get bushy. Pinching is great to help avoid tall thin plants. Try it on petunias, flowering tobacco, pansies, flowering maples, and geraniums to get really floriferous plants. But back to stakes. When necessary—and before your lanky plant blows over—insert at the base a sturdy bamboo pole as tall as the plant is projected to reach. Use yarn, string, or twist-ties every 10", attaching it first to the stake and then around the plant stem. Sometimes I use tree branches with a "Y" joint (like one you'd use to make a sling-shot) and simply prop up a droopy plant. This kind of staking is barely noticeable. You can also buy metal supports and hoops. These are useful for top-heavy flowers such as peonies, which too often display their blossoms in the mud.

DEADHEADING, SHAPING, AND PRUNING

Most plants need grooming. The most common cleanup is deadheading, which has nothing to do with concerts. It's simply cutting or pinching off faded blossoms and their stems. The technique varies. For a Shasta daisy, for example, take off the flower and its long stem where it emerges from the base of leaves. For a begonia, just pinch off the spent flower. Deadheading encourages plants to keep blooming rather than putting their energies into seed production. Sometimes the entire plant is cut back to persuade it to regenerate and re-bloom. These summer cutbacks are for June bloomers that look tired and worn out in July. Now's your chance to do some serious whacking, cutting back many perennials by half or more—sometimes all the way to the ground. A list of candidates that prosper after a cutback (and a subsequent feeding) include many daisies, meadow sage, lupine, columbine, and catmint.

You can always do a bit of shaping and pruning when you like, but most people do too much. For most of us, early spring is the best time to cut out dead branches on trees and shrubs and do minimal shaping. This is also the time to cut back perennials and ornamental grasses. Meadows can simply be mowed. The old idea that the garden needs to be put to bed in fall has pretty much gone by the wayside. Save your autumnal energy for planting bulbs and moving pots of tropical plants inside. Nowadays we leave perennials, grasses, and even some annuals alone as winter comes, the better to enjoy their freeze-dried beauty. This also helps to protect the crowns of the plants from the extremes of winter.

■ Tips to Save Energy: Yours and the Garden's

The rhythm of a garden isn't a constant one. Nor is a gardener's. In spring most of us have energy to burn. That's good because there's plenty to be accomplished. Last year's perennials and grasses are cut back in mid- to late winter, depending on where you live. At about the same time, cool-season annuals and vegetables need to be sown outdoors. Peas, for example, are traditionally planted on St. Patrick's Day across the northern tier of states. In the meantime, many gardeners get a jump on the growing season by starting warm-season annuals and vegetables indoors.

The weather plays us like a yo-yo. It's too cold. Then it's warming up. No, wait—it's still too cold. Well, it feels pretty mild; maybe I should start transplanting and spading the vegetable patch. Oops, it's snowing. The moisture was good anyway. Now maybe it's okay. It was still pretty chilly last night. It's been 90 degrees for a week now. Oh dear, is it too late to plant tomatoes? This weather roller coaster can really wear you down. In the beginning of the season (spring, that is) we all invariably overdo it. We're not yet garden tough, so sore muscles and strained backs become common. Our bodies tone and strengthen as the season progresses. By mid-June, we're feeling pretty buff.

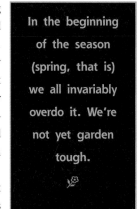

In the beginning of the season (spring, that is) we all invariably overdo it. We're not yet garden tough.

Then it hits. The heat, humidity, grasshoppers, and crabgrass start to take their toll. We've reached the summer energy crisis. In what's supposed to be the time when we most enjoy our gardens, we can become too worn out. It seems only the super-gardener can shrug off the summer's setbacks to keep his or her garden picture-perfect. I'm no super-gardener, but my midsummer garden looks pretty cool. Here's how:

- Water plants in early morning, deeply and only when necessary (remember, poke your fingers into the soil to see how much moisture your plants have).
- Count on container plantings for color and substance (these are the plants you can most easily control); use tropicals and other heat lovers.
- Give your plants plenty of food and water (especially for the container plantings); install drip lines in the garden if you're mechanically inclined.
- Cut back early-blooming perennials.
- Select a different, small area to be groomed each day. Give it 20 minutes or whatever time you can. Move on to a new area the next day.
- Wear light-colored clothing along with broad-brimmed hats when you garden.
- Don't sweat the small stuff, such as deadheading. There's always next week.
- The best time to pull a weed is when you see it.

■ Essential Garden Tools

What tools do you need? Forgive me if I say, "It depends." There are some perfectly nice tools I've never used, so I can only tell you what I find "essential" and "nice to have." Let's start with the ones I use most. The Japanese fisherman's knife, called a hori-hori, features a 7" steel blade, serrated on one side, with a wood or plastic handle. Its primary uses include weeding, planting small stuff, and, presumably, gutting fish. A hori-hori costs about $20 to $35 depending on the model you get. Only one major caveat: Keep this tool out of reach of your children!

PRUNERS AND LOPPERS

The next essential is a pair of pruners, also called secauters by people who don't think pruners is descriptive enough. There are several different styles. I'd suggest a basic pair with a grip that feels comfortable. You'll get plenty of use out of a pair of pruners when you cut back the garden in spring, prune shrubs and small tree branches, deadhead flowers, and harvest herbs. I'd splurge and get a good pair (meaning, lifetime), for which you'll spend close to $50. Loppers are like bigger pruners and can handle slightly larger limbs up to about 1 ½" in diameter. They're nice to have around (I borrow my neighbors'). You can get a decent lopper for about $30.

DIGGING TOOLS

Still in the essentials, you need a spade or shovel (unless you're a rooftop gardener and never dig in the earth). The classic shovel is for digging. Buy a good quality one that won't break when you do something dumb like pry a boulder out with it. Of course, now you say you wouldn't do anything like that—but you will. You can buy a decent shovel at the hardware store for $15 and up. A rubber coating at the end of the handle may help prevent blisters. A spade has a flat spade. I like my "border" spade a lot. It cost about $50, and I'll probably have it forever. I mainly use it for dividing: once you've dug up a big clump of daylilies or whatever, a good thrust with the blade will cut it cleanly in half. For people of petite stature, try a lady's spade, which is a smaller version, or a border spade, which is pretty much the same thing. I like this tool for working in tight quarters to dig holes for bulbs or new perennials.

I also get good use from my digging fork. It looks a bit like a pitchfork, but has longer, thinner tines and is much lighter. A digging fork is a sturdy tool, usually with four or five steel tines that are designed to loosen a vegetable garden's soil before planting or to lift clumps of perennials for transplanting or dividing. A cheap version of this tool will bend when confronted by heavy, wet soil, hidden rocks or debris, or a really entrenched shrub rose that you've decided to move. So do invest in a better tool that will stand the test of time.

Since we're still discussing digging tools, I'd also spring for a good-quality trowel. Essentially a miniature, hand-held spade, a trowel is designed for digging small holes for things like perennials and annuals. A good strong handle and sturdy blade are necessary. You'll bend a cheap one in two days. The point of contention is where the handle meets the blade. If this isn't securely joined, it will fall apart. One-piece forged pieces of stainless steel get around this problem. Be prepared to pay at least $25 for a good trowel.

I occasionally use my dibble, which is a quaint tool for making uniform holes for seeds or small bulbs. It's essentially a pointed, plump piece of wood (like a swollen wooden carrot) that you can probably live without. But it does look picturesque on the potting bench. Speaking of which, do you need a proper potting bench? I admire the really nice ones immensely, with their stainless-steel tops and compartments for potting soil and stuff. I usually do my seeding on the dining table or kitchen floor and I plant my containers in place on the patio or balcony. Still, a potting bench would look really stylish in my sunroom.

RAKES

Most people rake more than I do; I lack the obsession to remove every leaf and blade of grass that falls. When I had a lawn, I used a mulching mower (which I highly recommend) to chop up the leaves in my last fall mowing. I leave most leaves where they fall in the garden itself to protect plants and disintegrate over the winter. This is a judgment call, because too many leaves can compact into a slimy mess that smothers rather than protects your plants. But

Even when its days of service are over, a leaky wheelbarrow positioned by the tool shed holds a bevy of beautiful daylilies, liatris, and 'Moonbeam' coreopsis.

to the subject of rakes: a lightweight, aluminum leaf rake is pretty much indispensable around your property (you can get back-saving ergonomic models, as you can with many kinds of tools as well as those for lefties). Even better for working among plants in fall or spring is a rake with rubber tines that won't tear up your perennials. A small hand rake really comes in handy for tight spots.

A heavy iron garden rake gets most of its use in the vegetable garden for leveling and smoothing after digging. I often turn the head upside down to get rid of dirt clods by beating them with it. I'm not kidding; it's the best way.

HOES

Not everyone needs a hoe. I use a standard type, mainly for making furrows for planting seeds of corn, beans, and other vegetables. I used to have an old hoe that must have been in the garage when I bought the house. Poorly designed and constructed, the blade would occasionally fly off the handle. I was doing some serious weeding one day, chopping out clumps of grass and clover, when the flying-off-the-handle episodes became more frequent and dangerous.

So get a quality hoe that will stay in one piece. Another hoe I use more frequently is the "action" or "shuffle" hoe, which has a thin sharp blade on a hollow head that shuffles back and forth, and which cuts small weeds off just below the soil surface.

HOSES AND GARDEN MISCELLANY

Even if you put in an automated underground irrigation system, you'll still need a hose. Few things in gardening cause as much cussing as a hose that kinks. You'll pay more for a quality hose, but, again, you'll keep your cool. Get one longer than you think you'll need. A 50' hose is shorter than you imagined.

Among the things I use on a constant basis are plastic spray bottles (for soap sprays), a plastic ten-gallon bucket for toting tools and collecting garden debris, a hose reel for quick roll-ups, and various hose attachments. For container gardening, I use a watering wand with an adjustable head that I can dial up to get everything from a fine mist to a powerful jet. It's similar to the one you may have in your shower that pulses and massages. The advantage is that you can get a delicate spray so that you don't wash away seedlings, or a more aggressive spray for washing down the patio and everything in between.

Among the tools I've yet to find a use for are the hand claw (I don't think my plants would want me disturbing their roots on a daily basis) and the bulb planter, an aluminum tube that would be better for taking geological core samples if it weren't guaranteed to bring on carpal tunnel syndrome within three minutes of use. Surely I've had a few others that have long been buried in the back corners of the potting shed.

Once your relatives and friends see that you've become a gardener, you're bound to get garden stuff as gifts. If they garden, perhaps they'll give you useful things like pots and tools. Try to steer them in the right direction so that they don't give you trinkets like pink flamingos and resin plaques that say "My Garden" or "Squirrel Crossing."

■ Start to Plant!

At some point you'll need to stop reading, quit planning, and go buy some plants. Get yourself to your local nursery. Ask for help. Try not to get distracted by every pretty flower you see. Follow your list just like at the grocery store. There are plenty of suggestions within the regional section of this book, which immediately follows this introduction.

Part of being a good gardener is being a good observer. Watch what happens in your garden through the seasons and learn from it. As your thumb starts to get a little green glow, branch out and try new things. If you do indeed kill a plant (and you will), figure out why. Plants want to live, so something went wrong. The answer is usually that the plant received too much or too little water. Always poke your finger in the soil several inches deep before you water. If it's moist, hold off.

You're off and running. Take some classes. Read some more books. Get dirty.

Section 2

Your Northeast Garden

■ Getting Down and Dirty: Your Soil

ardeners joke about playing in the dirt, yet soil is critical to our success in growing anything we plant. Many beginners become enthused, run to the nursery, buy and plant many wonderful plants, only to have them not perform well. The only way to have a rewarding garden is to have good soil.

The soil in our gardens or in containers must provide a place for the roots to anchor the plant as they grow, spread out, and reach down. The roots search for nutrients and water, which good soil holds in the right proportion.

EVALUATING AND USING THE SOIL YOU HAVE

It is much easier and more logical to grow the types of plants that will do well in your existing soil. If your soil has decent drainage, try to adapt your ideas to what you have. If your soil is heavier with more clay content, try growing moisture-loving plants. If it is sandy, use

---

Cool colors of iris, lamb's ears, borage, and scabiosa flowers combine well in this sunny spot.

67

more succulents, herbs, and other plants that do not require high moisture. If you have acidic soil, as most of us in the Northeast do, grow acid-loving plants.

One simple way to evaluate your soil is to drop a shovelful of slightly moist soil on a concrete slab or hard surface. See how well it holds together upon impact. Your soil is too sandy if it totally falls apart; you will have to add more organic matter. If you have large chunks of soil or one big lump, it is mostly clay; you will have to add gritty material, coarse sand (not fine sand), and organic matter. The third possibility is soil in many small pieces of about the same size. That soil structure is good for many different types of plants and is the desired type for garden use.

Good garden soil crumbles easily; it is described as "friable" soil. A soil that clumps heavily is not good for plants. Sandy soil that will not hold together at all is not ideal either. Think of how water runs right through beach sand. Sand consists of larger particles that have a lot of space between them and hold little water. However, the soil should have some open pockets of air. If most of the particles are very small, as they are in clay, they all fit tightly together and there is no room left for air. Clay soil holds too much water and plants will drown. The roots will rot and your plants will die. You want a soil structure that is in between these extremes.

The third major component of soil is humus, organic matter from leaves and other plant material that falls to the ground and decomposes over a long period of time. Microorganisms live and work in the humus, creating nutrients that plants absorb through their roots. Much of what we do to improve the soil is to increase the level of humus so that the microorganisms can do more work and plants can have more nutrients available; this is called amending the soil. Organic matter also helps hold soil together.

Easy-to-grow miscanthus, rudbeckia, and 'Autumn Joy' sedum perform well in most soils.

Acidity of the Soil

Soil pH is the measure of relative acidity and alkalinity of soil. It is expressed as a number between 1 and 14, with 7 considered neutral, lower numbers indicating acidity, and higher numbers designating alkalinity. Decent garden soils range from around 4 (acid) to about 8.5 (alkaline); typical soils are closer to 7 (neutral).

This number is important because certain plants perform best in soil with a specific pH. Rhododendrons, azaleas, and hollies prefer acidic soil; blueberries demand alkaline soil. There are simple soil test kits available at nurseries, or you can take soil samples and pay the local extension service to test them.

To reduce the acidity of soil, add ground limestone. It takes about four pounds of limestone to raise pH from 5.5 to 6 in an area of 10' by 10'. To raise a pH of 5.0 to 5.5 in the same size area, apply eight pounds of ground limestone. In New England, the soil is generally somewhat acidic. If your soil is the same as your neighbors', look at what plants they are growing and you will probably be able to grow the same types.

Drainage Issues

To determine your soil's drainage capability, test how fast water will seep through the soil. This is called a percolation test. Dig a few holes 1' deep by 2' wide in areas you intend to garden. Cover the holes with plastic and let the soil dry out, then fill them with water and time how long it takes for the water to completely drain. Write this down. The ideal drainage time is 10 to 30 minutes.

If the water drains more quickly than 10 minutes, add organic matter so that the soil retains more moisture. If it drains more slowly, up to four hours, it will still probably work, although you will need to be careful to allow water to soak into the ground slowly so plants are watered adequately.

If the water takes longer than four hours to percolate, you may have a layer of hardpan, almost like concrete, some distance beneath the surface. This hard layer is preventing normal drainage of water. Try to locate it by digging with a posthole digger. Another simple test is to walk the area where you want to garden, holding a metal rod that you push into the soil at regular intervals. If you keep encountering hard resistance, remove soil to the hardpan level and break it up with sturdy hand tools or a tiller.

IMPROVING YOUR SOIL

Virtually all soils can be improved by the addition of organic matter. Typically, a 3" or 4" layer dug into the top 10" is best. This will make the soil texture better, help its water-holding capability, and provide more nutrients for your plants. Most of the following soil amendments are available in 20- to 40-pound bags at your local nursery. Some can be purchased in bulk or by the truckload, which you might want to consider for a large project. Try to purchase bags and bulk organic materials after a dry spell. Bags that have been stored indoors are fine, but most are stacked in the open. Organic matter absorbs water and gets very heavy after rains. Also, sometimes sprinklers at a nursery spray water on the bags. Following are some organic components to consider.

Compost is the end product of allowing dead plant parts to decay: leaves, grass clippings, vegetable scraps, wood chips, soil, and so on. It may include small wood pieces, which will continue to break down in the garden. If you will be buying a lot of compost, check different brands and select the best texture, which should be soft and springy to the touch. Large quantities can be purchased by the truckload from commercial sources and are sometimes available from your municipality; call to find out what materials are composted in your area. A 40-pound bag should cover one square yard to the depth of 3".

Composted manure has good soil-improving qualities and adds nitrogen to the soil, although the amount will vary greatly between cow, chicken, and other manures. For large-animal manure, generally allow one 40-pound bag spread 1" deep over 3 square yards. Follow application rates on bags for stronger manure.

Humus can be made from a range of organic items: sawdust, wood chips, leaves, and top soil. Buy one bag each of several different brands to determine if you like the texture, color, and smell, then use more of the best one. A 40-pound bag should cover 2 square yards to the depth of 2" to 3".

Peat moss is harvested from peat bogs in Canada and Michigan, is quite acidic, and holds a lot of water. Some gardeners are concerned that we are removing too much of it from bogs, so they opt to use other materials. Peat moss is best used to improve sandy soils, not as mulch.

Topsoil varies tremendously. Buy one bag each of different brands to determine which one you prefer. For a large project, get soil samples first so that you can select the best one. The coverage rates will be somewhere between those of humus and compost.

MAKING YOUR OWN COMPOST

Composting is simple and rewarding. It produces usable material to improve your soil and decreases the amount of garbage that is hauled away from your home.

Organic materials can simply be layered on top of each other on the ground. Many people prefer a more orderly approach, and put the materials into a semi-enclosed structure or a commercial composter. A simple three-sided box will work fine, or add a hinged door that swings open. You can make one with wooden pallets, snow fencing, or metal fencing. To allow air circulation, it is best to construct the bin of a material that is about 50 percent open on the sides.

For the fastest decomposition, select a site in full sun. Layer different types of organic matter by color: green on the bottom (plant and fresh grass clippings if you do not have a mulching mower); then brown (fall leaves); then black (soil); and finally colors (vegetable and fruit waste). During warm weather, compost will just happen. Building the compost pile using small particles or shredded components and turning it once a week will also produce compost more quickly. Keep the pile slightly moist and turn it over, mixing the layers with a garden fork when you have the energy. As you build the pile, make it no larger than 3' by 4' and leave a depression in the center to make adding moisture easier. Add a handful of nitrogen fertilizer to speed decay.

Some gardeners like to use a series of three matching compost bins attached side-by-side. The first bin holds the fresh material. Once it is somewhat decomposed, move it into the second bin, then into the third when it is fully composted. Use finished compost in your garden.

WORKING THE SOIL

In the past, gardeners would attack their soil each spring, tilling it with a machine or turning it by hand. Today's experts think we should turn the soil as little as possible. The exception is your first garden, although you can eliminate much of the heavy work if you plan your garden well in advance and use the following techniques (we will discuss planting later in the

COMPOSTING DOs AND DON'Ts

DO COMPOST: coffee grounds, eggshells, fruit and vegetable scraps, grass clippings, flowerheads (without seeds), leaves, manure, paper (black printing only, shredded is best), plant clippings, sawdust, and soil.

DON'T COMPOST: Bones, carnivore feces, diseased plants, fats and oils, seedheads, or meat. ■

book). If possible, prepare beds in the fall so you can start working in your garden very early the next spring.

Before starting, dig down several feet into the soil to determine if there are any major problems, such as a layer of hardpan, rock, or a very wet area that might require tile installation for drainage. You may opt to have the bed tilled rather than digging it yourself. It does eliminate work, but you should do it infrequently as it can lead to the creation of a hardpan layer. It is particularly important to use a tiller if you are doing a large area. In most places, you can rent or borrow one.

Be very careful not to work soil when it is wet. It is also best not to step on wet soil or soil components. This will compact it and ruin the structure and texture of the soil, eliminating the aeration and ultimately destroying useful bacteria and organisms. A simple test to determine if soil can be safely worked is to take a handful of soil and squeeze it together. Tap that ball of soil with your finger. Soil that is ready to work breaks apart easily. If the soil stays together in a clump, it is too wet and you should allow it to dry out more. If it does not hold together at all, the soil is too dry. Water that area and wait a day or so, then repeat the test.

No-Dig Gardening

Try this approach in a relatively small area, as it requires a lot of organic matter. Start with a planting bed no larger than 10' by 10' or 5' by 20', although smaller might be better. In an area that has been lawn, cut the grass as close to the ground as possible, leaving all clippings in place. Water the area thoroughly. Layer 2" to 4" of organic matter over your planting bed. As you add more layers, moisten each one. Lay down a ½" thick layer of newspapers (black and white printing only) or cardboard, then moisten. Add a 4" layer of compost or peat moss (about 14 bags of commercial compost). Add a layer of shredded green matter or yard waste, and then repeat the compost/peat moss layer. It's best to add layers until they reach a minimum depth of 18". Let this bed settle for about a week, and then you can plant in it.

Traditional Cultivation

Remove a 3" deep layer of grass in the area you wish to plant. (Use the grass to patch other areas of your lawn or reserve it, chop it up, and use it in the compost pile.) Start by digging on one side of the bed to remove one spade width and depth of the soil across the length of the area, piling it in a wheelbarrow or on a tarp. Then slice off the next row to the same depth, rolling the soil into the open space. Break up that soil with your spade, then continue to repeat the process until the last row of soil is removed, turned, and broken up. Place the soil that you had set aside from the first part of the digging into that final open trench. Add any organic matter and amendments required, then dig them into the bed. Continue to break up any chunks of soil as you go, then rake the surface until it is smooth. For the flattest surface, turn a metal rake over and use the back side to finish the process. This type of preparation is adequate for most annuals and vegetables.

Double-Digging

Double-digging is a better approach for plants that need more root space and will be in that location for a long time, such as roses, peonies, and other perennials. It is also one of the most physically demanding gardening tasks ever invented as it requires a huge amount of digging.

Remove the grass as just described, then remove a 1' wide and one spade depth row of soil across the length of the bed and reserve it for later use. Then break up the subsoil in that same trench, going down another 10". Use a garden fork to break up the subsoil and to dig in amendments. Working in the trench, move the next row of topsoil into the trench and break that up, then the subsoil in the same area. Continue doing this across the bed. At the last row, you will add the soil reserved from the first row. Finish the bed as above.

Raised Beds

Raised beds are like a big, sturdy window box on the ground. You can construct them with water-resistant woods or other materials, including bricks, staked logs, vertical timbers, or railroad ties. Do not make them more than 3' by 4' if you are tall, so that you can easily reach all areas of the bed. They should be at least 6" deep; 9" is better. Loosen the topsoil with a digging fork. Then add soil, compost, and other amendments to fill the box. Water and allow the mixture to settle for several days before planting.

PLANTING

Planting seems intimidating the first few times you do it. Actually, it is quite simple, easy, and fun to do. It's a good idea to start with small annuals purchased in pots. All plants have a best side, just as people do. Before planting, hold the plant at eye level and turn it until the best side faces front.

Use a hand trowel to create a planting hole in your prepared bed that is somewhat wider than the rootball but equal in depth to its container; set the soil aside as you remove it. The rootball is the entire area where the plant roots are holding together, generally about the full size of the pot. To remove the plant from the pot, tap the pot against a hard surface or tap the pot gently with your hand trowel. This loosens the plant so you can easily remove it from the pot. Tip the pot so the plant hangs down; then shake the plant out of the pot. Hold it by the rootball,

---

TRANSPLANTING SHRUBS AND TREES FROM CONTAINERS

1. Dig a hole the same depth as the rootball and two to three times as wide; reserve the soil on a tarp. Use a stick or the same size container to measure the depth (the soil line to the bottom of the pot).

2. Tap the container to loosen the rootball; cut off any roots growing through drainage holes that prevent removing the plant from the pot.

3. Place the plant in the hole with its best side to the front; make sure the plant is vertical and not leaning over. Backfill the hole with reserved and improved soil.

4. Double-check that the plant is vertical, then tamp the soil in place.

5. Create a "donut" of soil several inches high and just larger than the width of the rootball.

6. Water slowly over time, using a trickle from the hose, until the rootball is moistened. Continue to water by hand over a period of months or years. An older tree or shrub will take years to become established.

7. Add 2" to 3" (more is not better) of organic mulch over the excavated area. Keep the mulch a few inches away from the trunk of the plant.

8. Stake trees with thin trunks or those planted in windy locations; others develop more strongly without ties or stakes. ∎

This front yard conifer garden is a diverse mix of textures, colors, shapes, and heights and is a no-mow alternative to grass.

not the plant, and place it into the center of the planting hole. If the rootball seems to be a tight mass of roots, you need to tease the roots out with your fingers. If they are so tight that separating them is impossible, make several vertical cuts with a sharp, clean knife through the outside roots in several places around the pot. Do this without breaking the rootball apart.

Place the rootball into the prepared hole. Return some of the reserved soil into the space between the rootball and the sides of the hole. Press that soil in place with your fingers or a stick, and then water well and slowly so that the entire area around the rootball is moistened. If you are planting a number of plants in the same area, plant them all, then water. If a single plant wilts (the foliage becomes limp), water that individual plant. It is a good idea to water small plants in their containers the day before planting, large plants a couple of days before.

Large plants, perennials, shrubs, and trees are planted much the same way, although their size can be a challenge. Watch how you handle all heavy objects: use proper lifting techniques, and get help to move large plants. They can weigh hundreds of pounds.

WATERING

Plants require varying amounts of water to meet their individual needs; not too much or too little or a standard amount every week. It is important to understand your soil, the impact of weather, and the needs of particular plants. Plants will show you when they desperately need water by drooping. Unfortunately, they may droop the same way if they have too much water.

Keep an eye on your soil and notice how the color changes with different rainfall levels. The higher the temperature, the more moisture will leave the soil and plants through transpiration. If you have sandy soil and hot temperatures, you will need to water more often than if you have clay-based soils at low temperatures. Consider the extreme example of bog plants compared to desert plants. Bog plants and other moisture-loving plants want soil that is constantly moist. Desert plants—cacti and succulents—need little water because they give off only small amounts of moisture through transpiration and are equipped to go long periods between rainfalls. Most plants are somewhere in between. Learn the needs of each of the plants you grow and water them accordingly. It is also best to group plants together that have similar water needs.

You want water to get to the roots of plants. Although it is expedient to use sprinklers to water a large area, sprinklers really work best for lawns. Water is a precious resource and everyone should learn how to use it wisely. Custom watering by hand is more effective for plants. The ideal technique is applying water in a way that it slowly drips, then seeps into the rootzone of plants. This can be done with a hose that is allowed to run slowly in a specific location or a soaker hose that keeps the water near the rootzone.

You should water early in the day so that plants can dry off before nightfall, preventing the spread of many diseases. This is also the cool part of the day, so less water will evaporate before reaching the plant. Remember, too, that the surface of the soil must be moistened before any water can be absorbed and penetrate the soil.

FERTILIZER

Plants need a variety of nutrients to grow and thrive. Much like humans, they need a balanced "diet" to do well. For plants, there are three major nutrients called "macronutrients," along with trace elements needed in much smaller quantities. Good organic soils will supply most of your plants' needs, although supplementation with fertilizer can improve their performance.

The three major nutrients that make up a "complete" food are: nitrogen (N), phosphorus (P), and potassium (K). Fertilizer packages always list those nutrients in that order with a percentage given for each. For instance, a 10-pound bag of 10-15-20 would contain 1 pound of nitrogen, 1.5 pounds of phosphorus, and 2 pounds of potassium.

WHEN TO FERTILIZE

LAWNS—spring and fall

TREES AND SHRUBS—after three years of growth and no later than three months prior to last frost date

PERENNIAL FLOWERS—when growth resumes in the spring and no later than two months

prior to last frost date

ANNUAL FLOWERS AND VEGETABLES—add time-release fertilizer to soil when planting and fertilize periodically through growing season

ROSES—modern hybrids every three weeks, antique roses once per year ∎

In this small border, hosta and heuchera foliage and flowers contrast nicely, accented by a casual rock wall that separates them from the lawn.

Nitrogen tends to produce foliage growth. A nitrogen-heavy fertilizer might be a 20-5-5 blend. If you give plants too much nitrogen, they will produce very lush foliage at the expense of flowers or fruit. Nitrogen can also burn the roots, so it is always better to use too little fertilizer as opposed to too much. Nitrogen is also the least stable fertilizer component and can leach through the soil into the surrounding environment.

Phosphorus promotes the growth of roots, flowers, and fruit. A low dose of high-phosphorus fertilizer is good to use with transplants of all kinds. Potassium is also important in helping the plant absorb other nutrients and seems to help in the absorption of water. It also aids photosynthesis and immunity to disease, so it is a nutrient critical to overall plant health.

Learn how much fertilizer your plants need; some are heavy feeders, some are not. For example, roses need a lot of fertilizer; but most wildflowers and herbs do best without it. Use fertilizers only when they are needed and generally apply at rates less than their labels instruct.

THE MAGIC OF MULCH

Organic mulches break down over time and add nutrients to the soil, in effect acting as slow-release fertilizers. They can include bark chips, compost, leaf mold, pine needles, saw dust, or straw. All mulches block light so weed seeds have a harder time starting. They also soften the pounding of rain so soil does not wash away, and they even prevent diseases from splashing from the ground onto leaves. They also help to keep rootzones cooler in the summer and

**LEFT: Bellflowers, lamb's ears, and 'Bressingham Purple' alumroot create a cool color vignette.
RIGHT: Pachysandra and azaleas are a calm green presence for most of the year—
at least until the azaleas erupt into brilliant early spring color.**

maintain consistent freezing temperatures in winter. This helps avoid heaving, when plants pop up and sometimes out of the soil because of fluctuating temperatures.

Inorganic mulches can include gravel, plastic sheeting, landscape fabric, and old carpeting. In a rock garden or herb garden, you may choose gravel or pebbles; in a perennial border, you might choose compost or leaf mold. In more visible areas of the garden, you will probably choose something more attractive than old carpeting. Fresh wood chips deplete the soil of nitrogen, so you need to use a supplemental nitrogen fertilizer at the time of application.

Generally, a 2" to 4" layer of mulch will be effective. If mulch is heavy or dense, use far less. You can use more of lightweight mulches like straw. Use mulch in the spring after the ground has warmed and plants have resumed growing. The one exception to this rule is black plastic mulch, which will help the ground warm more quickly. The warm ground helps plants get a good start before placing organic mulch around them. This also helps small plants and seedlings grow so you avoid smothering them as you want to do with the weeds.

Apply winter mulch after the soil freezes. Add this to any remaining summer mulch. The best type is a lightweight mulch like straw that can be applied from 6" to 12" deep. The final depth of mulch depends on how cold your area gets, the needs of specific plants, and the type of mulch you use. Cold-sensitive plants will need more protection and more mulch.

Do not pile mulch or soil high up against the trunk of a tree or shrub so it looks like a volcanic mountain. Mulch should be spread out 2" to 4" thick over the rootball of the plant. None should touch the trunk.

■ Design Choices

In order to decide the style of garden you desire and then choose features and plants you want, you should think about how you will use your property. There are some practical considerations such as how you play, entertain, dine, or relax in your garden. Consider the needs of your children and pets. Do you want some of the following?

A hideaway—you may want a spot or several spots where you can retreat from your busy life and world. How about a quiet area to sit and listen to birds or the trickle of water and sip iced tea or read a book?

A cutting garden—do you want lots of fresh flowers in your house? Think of growing bright, cheery flowers to cut throughout the season.

Entertainment space—will you be inviting small or large groups of people over to celebrate occasions, dine, or party? Do you need an intimate space or more room for fun?

Recreation—do you want a tennis court, swimming or lap pool, or space for croquet or to toss a football with your kids?

Bountiful vegetables—do you have the urge to grow lots of heirloom tomatoes, cucumbers, and squash for eating fresh, freezing, or canning?

Herb garden—do you want lots of fresh herbs for cooking or drying? Do you need a large amount of garden space, or will a few containers supply all you need?

Storage—where are you going to put all the outdoor toys, garden tools, barbecue grill and tools, propane tanks, firewood, or hoses?

Privacy—do you need to block a neighbor's view of your property and gardens?

THE PLANNING PROCESS

In order to help you plan, try this exercise: quickly write down as many things as you can that you want your garden to do for you. Set that list aside, read this entire chapter, and then repeat the exercise a few days later. Then compare and study the lists and select the three most important items from your lists. Have your spouse do the same exercise, then discuss and combine your top choices.

Whatever your choices, they are yours and are far more likely to make you happy in the long run. This is your garden, one you will live with for years to come; make it uniquely your own. Think of a landscape as all facets of your property, including all the hardscape elements. Then collect plants to use within that overall plan.

Now factor in time. How much time do you have to maintain your landscape and where do you want to utilize it? Some garden types require much more maintenance than others. Lawns need mowing every week during the growing season. To save time, use more ground covers or deck and patio space. Informal mixed shrub borders need little care except occasional pruning; formal hedges need to be pruned regularly, maybe twice per year. Some trees are messier than others; deciduous trees drop all their leaves; and fruit trees may be a positive or negative, depending on your desires. Flower borders need intense work in spring and often again in fall.

Along with determining how you will use your space—for example, an area for lawn games, a swimming pool, a vegetable or herb garden, and patio or deck for cooking and entertaining—you need to know how you look at your garden. Do you want your best view from the house;

say, the kitchen or dining room windows? Will you spend most of your time on your deck or patio and view the garden from there?

Balance your desires, time, and budget carefully. Spend your dollars and time on the things that matter most to you. If you can, have others do jobs you do not enjoy, like mowing the lawn. It is also wise to start small, with a manageable border or bed; add more as your budget and time allow. Make it fun. Gardening should not become a chore.

ANALYZE YOUR SITE

Before you add or build new features, you need to understand what your property is like. Start by mapping out the entire property, including the house, other structures, decks, patios, fences, trees, shrubs, and borders. Understand that creating your landscape is a large and expensive undertaking that may entail more than just adding some plants. You need to plan the major elements very carefully, as you will live with and pay for them for years. Create a drawing of your existing property to scale. A survey map might be a good place to begin. It is best to measure the size of and distances between all key elements and draw them to scale.

If all of this seems daunting, you may wish to consult a professional who will help you create the plan. This plan, like your own, can be executed in stages. The investment in professional help could prevent costly errors. It is easy to move a few annuals, or even perennials, but think of the difficulty and expense of moving a large tree, a deck, or a swimming pool that you discover is not in the correct place.

Here are things to note on your landscape map:

Existing hardscape—walls, fences, decorative structures, patios, and decks.

Existing plants—trees, shrubs, and ground covers that are likely to remain.

Sun and shade—light patterns throughout the day and seasons (remember that deciduous trees lose their leaves in winter and allow more sun through), and shade from trees and structures, including your neighbors.

Wind—strong winds that affect plant health and people comfort.

Soil types—note the range of soil types, particularly their texture, moisture-holding capacity, and pH.

Views—include all views that you want to borrow or hide.

Once you have your needs determined and all your significant features drawn to scale, do a few rough drafts of a plan. Make several copies of the scale drawing and sketch in the

Container gardens can stand alone or fill in empty spots in a border, adding color or height as needed.

major use areas of your landscape. Keep moving things around until you reach a comfort level with the plan. This will take several attempts, so do not worry when the first plan is less than perfect.

Feel free to show your plan to others and have them comment. They may notice problems that you had not considered. Then refine your plan some more and create a long-term action plan. Decide which parts of the overall plan need to be done first and what your budget is for each major step, along with the total for the whole project. Remember that the most permanent features and plants should be installed first: hardscape and trees, then shrubs, perennials, and annuals. If your budget only allows hardscape features the first year, fill in with annuals for color.

GARDEN STRUCTURE: DEM BONES, DEM BONES

The structure of a garden is called "bones" by professionals. Think of what the garden will look like in winter with the flowers and many of the plants dormant, perhaps with a coat of white snow to accentuate the lines. Strong lines create bones. Walks, walls, hedges, fences, and linear plantings make up the lines of a garden. It's easy to understand how the hardscape does this, but what about the plants? Perhaps a hedge is the easiest to visualize—many plants of an evergreen shrub carefully shaped into a strong straight line of green. Or, visualize a row of mixed shrubs creating a softer, yet important line or axis through the garden. Also consider a row of trees or beds of distinct shapes, often rectangular. These all help to create strong lines through your garden. Often there is a visual element, a piece of sculpture or some other focal point to draw your eye through these lines toward the very end of that sight line.

When you have finished your own landscape plan and drawing, examine it for strong lines. If you see few strong lines and do not have a vision of your garden in winter, it is a sign that you need to keep working on the plan in order to ensure it has strong bones.

FORMAL VERSUS INFORMAL DESIGN

What style of garden do you like best, formal or informal? Formal gardens have more symmetry and straight lines. They include a lot of rectangular shapes, often echoing each other from one side of the garden to the other or across a path. Pools, decks, and borders are designed with straight lines. Often there is some focal point, a piece of sculpture, sundial, or a birdbath that "pulls" your eye into that border or garden. Formal designs are somewhat easier to create as most people are used to working with straight lines.

Informal design has a lot of curving lines. Sidewalks gently bend around trees and structures; lawn, border, and pool edges curve. Informal does not mean haphazard or casual. The lines of the design will still need to be prominent, even if plant selection is lush or exuberant— maybe more so. Balance often is asymmetrical as opposed to symmetrical. You also can do a relaxed style of planting within a formal structure; this is often the best choice of all.

OUTDOOR ROOMS

One technique to help achieve strong bones and good design is to create outdoor rooms. The interior of your house is broken into distinct areas based on how you use them. You decorate each of those rooms with an individual style, linked to function and aesthetics. You can do the same thing outside; think in terms of outdoor rooms with walls, a floor, and a ceiling.

The floor of an outdoor room is the ground. It may be paved or covered by grass or a ground cover. The walls can be solid rock or wood walls, trellises covered in vines, or vertical plant materials that define the space. The ceiling can be a pergola, an arbor, or a patio umbrella. It also may be the sky itself framed by plant material.

Include all of your room ideas in your plan. This helps you focus your efforts and overall planning. That way you know if you have space for all the things you desire.

DECKS AND PATIOS

Your landscape plan should include your ideal deck and patio. Homeowners who create their own plans almost always underestimate the size of deck or patio they need. An old rule of thumb was to allow 125 square feet of space for each person in the house. Professionals now estimate that deck-patio square footage should equal at least one-third of the footprint of the house (i.e., the square feet of the house at ground level). As we do more and more outdoor living and entertaining, perhaps we should allow even more space. If the budget does not permit building it all the first year, use the future building space to plant annuals.

Deck materials include weather-resistant wood, pressure-treated wood, and new materials created from recycled items. Consider appearance, maintenance, cost, and life span of these materials before making a final decision. For all building projects, particularly for raised decking, pools, and water features, learn all the local zoning restrictions, permit requirements, and safeguards to protect you, your family, and friends.

Patio materials include local stone, paving stone, brick, and cement. Paving bricks are much more durable than those used for buildings; they also cost more and will last longer. Cement is a low-cost material that can be colored or textured to add interest.

Many building supply stores conduct seminars on building decks and patios. Carefully weigh the pluses and minuses of building these features yourself. Figure out the skills and time needed to do it yourself versus having a professional install it.

PATHS AND WALKWAYS

Paths through your landscape are important style features of your garden that add to the practical use and enjoyment of your property. Make sure that those terrific-looking lines on your

---

SHAPES OF TREES

COLUMNAR—tubular shape, several times higher than wide	SPREADING (horizontal spread)—several times wider than tall
CONE—shaped like a pine cone; triangular	VASE—Inverted triangular shape
FASTIGIATE—very narrow tubular shape, narrower than columnar	WEEPING—central trunk with branches weeping downward ■
GLOBE—rounded	

This secret garden creates a spot for quiet contemplation; its formal lines, textural green shrubs, and ground covers surround a sculptural focal point on a base of color.

paper plan are going in the direction people want to travel. If you have lived someplace for a few years, you will already know where people want to walk. What you will see are worn patches and lines through the grass, all those routes that have no sidewalk.

Plan the widths of walkways carefully; allow enough room for a wheelbarrow or other equipment to move down them. You should build paths at least 3' wide or 5' wide for a walkway that can accommodate two people walking side by side.

TREE DESIGN CONSIDERATIONS

SHAPE—as described on page 80

COLOR—leaf and needle color vary during the growing season; fall color can be yellow, red, and everything in between

FLOWERS—some trees have insignificant flowers; others have large and showy ones, like magnolias and crepe myrtles

FRAGRANCE—most trees have little fragrance; a few provide dramatic scent to the garden, like the fringe tree

BARK—some trees have spectacular bark that is visible in winter, like the mottled bark of stewartias or the peeling, polished red-brown color bark of the paperbark maple

FRUIT—edible or decorative fruit from such trees as apple, pear, and cherry is an asset or problem depending on your desires

TEXTURE—leaves vary from fine-needled shapes to large surfaces that reflect light, varying the textural quality of trees ■

**LEFT: This conifer collection provides privacy, color, and textural contrast year round and year after year.
RIGHT: A hot combination of annuals, pepper 'Chilly Chili' and 'New Look' celosia,
give a blast of color for one long season.**

The least expensive approach is packed soil. Frequently this is covered with landscape cloth or plastic, then bark chips or gravel. The least expensive permanent material is cement. If you are on a tight budget, think of ways to make the cement more exciting. You can add different types of stone, pebbles, or other aggregates into the mix. Color can be incorporated by using cement colors. Texture can be added with a stiff broom or metal rake. Plant leaves can also be pressed into the cement while it is slightly soft. Other items can be pressed into the surface of the cement for visual interest: marbles, pebbles, pottery shards, broken glass, or tiles. Brick, stone, wood, and recycled plastic are all used to create walkways.

SELECTING TREES

Trees are the most enduring of all the plants. Some can last for hundreds of years or even longer. They are the aristocrats of the garden, towering over other plant life, even over the house itself. For these reasons, you need to select the trees you will add to your landscape carefully. That cute little tree in a container can someday become a 100' tall giant of huge girth.

Investigate each tree you are considering. Learn the size of the tree at maturity, which is often very different from that of a young tree. Most trees in the nursery are labeled with this information. If the tree is not labeled with a Latin and cultivar name and complete information, do not buy it. Learn about the shape of the tree at maturity, the texture and color of its leaves through the seasons, along with the seeds or fruit produced by the tree. Some trees and shrubs are known to have weak wood and can split with heavy snowfall—for instance, Bradford pears.

Deciduous trees are those that lose their leaves in winter. Typical New England forests have many deciduous type trees: oaks, maples, and dogwoods. What we call evergreen trees are technically conifers that come in various shades of green, blue, silver, yellow, or gold. Although they do drop some needles (pines) or scale-like leaves (junipers) throughout the year, they maintain an "evergreen" appearance. Typical evergreen types include cedar, spruce, hemlock, juniper, pine, and fir. Dwarf conifers are smaller than the species. Some "dwarfs" are more than 50' tall, so be vigilant in checking the mature size of every tree you purchase.

Tall trees can shade a house, garage, or patio. Place a large deciduous tree so that it shades the house or patio during the summer. In winter, the tree will have dropped its leaves and allow the sun to warm the house. A large conifer in the same location would shade the structure year round, preventing the sun from natural warming. If you happen to have large, mature trees shading too much of your garden, you can have a professional arborist remove some of the branches and open up a tree to let more light shine into the areas you desire.

Remember that tree trimming, particularly any that requires a chainsaw or takes place in areas of a tree that you cannot reach from the ground should not be attempted by homeowners. This work requires special knowledge and is very dangerous if you are not thoroughly trained. Use professionally trained and certified arborists. In cities, most transportation departments and utility companies have regulations about which trees can be planted. These rules protect sight lines at intersections and lessen the chance of trees and limbs causing power outages during storms.

SELECTING SHRUBS

Shrubs are the core of most landscapes. They can be the size of small trees or just a few feet tall. As suburban lots shrink, shrubs have become even more important and may be substituted for trees. Some can be shaped to look like a tree. You should take the same care in selecting shrubs as you do trees and learn their mature size and value to your garden. They also can be deciduous or evergreen, such as needle conifers or broad-leafed evergreens like rhododendrons.

Shrubs have a range of attributes that add to our landscapes. Rhododendrons display large showy flowers in the spring as do pieris, corylopsis, viburnum, and fothergilla. Some have attractive berries for visual appeal or sustenance for birds and wildlife. They include: mahonia, callicarpa, viburnum, and pyracantha. Broad-leaved evergreens include rhododendron, boxwood, holly, and acuba; needle-type evergreen conifers include juniper, pine, plum yew, and Russian cypress.

Evergreen plants add color to your winter landscape. The tall ones might shade your house in winter, so plant them where that will not happen. Remember that evergreens do not shed their leaves in winter and thus need more water than deciduous plants. Through fall and winter, be diligent to water them when no rain supplies their moisture needs.

You always create a stronger visual statement by grouping three to five (or more in an odd number) specimens of the same shrub together. This is true for most plants. Look at examples in your area of gardeners who have planted one of everything. Compare that to someone who uses multiple plants, which creates a much stronger design.

You can combine shrubs with trees, layering larger plants in back, with a relaxed "stair step" arrangement to create a woodland or shade garden. Use large conifers in back of smaller deciduous shrubs so they will show through in winter.

FOUNDATION PLANTINGS

There are a few special issues you need to consider for your foundation plantings. Mature plant size is certainly a critical factor. How many times have you seen overgrown foundation plantings blocking views from windows and doors of the house and not allowing in light?

In urban areas, this can be a safety issue, when plants block views of your home's vulnerable areas. Under windows, choose a plant that naturally spreads horizontally or multiple low-growing shrubs planted in clusters. Use a similar strategy for plants along walkways that lead to front and back doors; both the mature width and height are significant issues in your choices. It is important to keep plants away from the house and out of walkways; this separation allows air to circulate and helps prevent moisture problems along the foundation and on the house. It also leaves room to work on your house for regular maintenance such as painting or window cleaning. By using plants that grow lower than the windows, you will avoid constant pruning.

Use a foundation planting that complements your house. Select evergreens and deciduous plants to give you variety. If you use mostly evergreens, you can add seasonal color by planting annuals in front of this area. A center hall colonial-style house will be more symmetrical and calls for a more formal and balanced design. A bungalow or ranch-style house will be less rigidly balanced and calls for a more relaxed planting scheme.

FLOWER BORDERS

Plan your flower border in the same fashion as you have done for the rest of your landscape. Sketch it on graph paper, placing plants where you would like them. Keep in mind that the taller plants go in the back and shorter ones in the front. You should plant in groups of three or more of a single kind of plant, allowing enough space for them to grow and mature. Create a plan that includes flowers that bloom early, midseason, and then in the late part of the season. You can concentrate the bloom to flourish at the time you will most use that part of the garden. Familiarize yourself with leaf color and texture as the foliage of these plants will be around for longer time periods than the flowers.

It is fine to copy a border plan right out of a book. You can make adjustments as you work on the border. Often a specific plant is not available when you are planting, so you substitute. Don't worry—enjoy the process and learn about the plants you select. You will find that some

LOW-GROWING SHRUBS

COMMON NAME	LATIN NAME	EVERGREEN/ DECIDUOUS	ZONE
Glossy abelia	*Abelia grandiflora*	E	Zones 6–9
Barberry	*Berberis thunbergii*	D	Zones 4–9
Boxwood	*Buxus microphylla japonica*	E	Zones 6–9
Fothergilla	*Fothergilla gardenii*	D	Zones 4–8
Holly	*Ilex verticillata* 'Red Sprite'	D	Zones 3–9
Juniper	*Juniperus horizontalis* cultivars	E	Zones 3–9
Plum yew	*Cephalotaxus harringtonia*	E	Zones 5–9
Rose	Knock Out varieties	D	Zones 4–9
Russian cypress	*Microbiota decussata*	E	Zones 3–8

plants are much nicer than you thought, while others will not perform as well as expected. If you do not like where something is in your garden, just move it.

Learn the needs of each of your plants. Do they benefit from pinching, or cutting the growing part of the stem back to a pair of leaves early in the season? Should you deadhead, removing the spent flowers before they become seedpods? Often this encourages a plant to flower another time during the season; it also prevents seeds from scattering all over your garden and germinating.

PERENNIALS

Herbaceous perennials, plants whose top growth dies to the ground each winter, are the backbone of flower borders. They provide color, structure, and foliage texture throughout the growing season and often persist for 20 years or more. There are selections for shade or sun and wet or dry conditions that will bloom in every color of the rainbow. Some are a few inches tall; others tower to 6' or 7' tall. Hostas, daylilies, and other favorites are described in some detail in our plant portrait section. Other sun-loving perennials to consider are asters, baby's breath, bee balm, black-eyed Susan, coreopsis, phlox, and yarrow.

Select perennials to suit the conditions that you have: shade or sun; rich organic soil or lean soil; and good drainage or wet conditions. Choose the mature height that works for you and colors that you like; some perennials are also fragrant. It is best to prepare the soil so that it is a rich, organic mix with adequate drainage as some of these plants will be in place for years. Other plants will need to be dug out of the border and divided every three, four, or five years.

ANNUALS

An annual is a plant that grows to maturity in one season, flowers, sets seed, and dies; a plant that lives its whole life within one year. We also treat other plants as annuals even though they are true perennials and will persist for years in warmer climates. This is true for many flowers, herbs, and vegetables. Think of these tender perennials as temporary plants.

When we think of annuals, we think of color, color, and more color. Often they start blooming early in the season and just keep at it until a killing frost. Frequently they have been planted in large beds that blast your senses with color. This is called "carpet bedding." Annuals tend to be low-maintenance plants that require only water and fertilizer to keep producing flowers.

Use annuals anyplace you would like color—in a mixed border, in their own beds, in containers, and to fill in spots anywhere some other plant has died or faded away. It is not cheating to run to the nursery, purchase a few annuals, and fill those empty spaces in your garden. So do not hesitate to do so before a family barbecue to make your garden look better.

Selecting annuals is a challenge, as there are so many good ones to choose from. Select the color, height, and shape of plants that work for you. For solid performance, look for guidance from knowledgeable local gardeners who love to share advice, and from award programs like the All-American Selections (AAS) program (see Resources). AAS has test gardens all over the United States where they grow and compare plants, giving their seal of approval to high-performance plants. Also, visit public gardens so you can see examples of well-grown plants at their best.

MIXED BORDERS

Many people today actually combine all types of plants into a decorative mixed border, including small trees, shrubs, perennials, annuals, vegetables, herbs, and tropical houseplants. The backbone of the border is the woody plants, trees and shrubs, both deciduous and coniferous, along with perennial flowers and herbs. Annuals and decorative vegetables, such as peppers, tomatoes, and herbs, can be planted in the border for extra color for a single season; but the core plants continue year after year.

The design process is similar to and should follow the basic guidelines described previously. Remember how a master plan for the entire landscape makes this an orderly process, helping you to move steadily toward a known result, avoiding major mistakes and costly errors. Often these borders evolve over a number of years, starting with a fence as backdrop. Small trees and shrubs are added over time. After the woody plants are in place, you start to fill in other plants. You have much more flexibility at that point; either follow your plan closely or substitute plants that you now desire more or that are new to the market. Your tastes will change over time. Generally, put the larger ones farther back, smaller in front, giving them plenty of room to reach their mature size. You likely will have large gaps between plants that will mature and fill in those spaces a number of years from now. For now, plant fast-growing annuals or perennials in the bare spots.

CONTAINER GARDENS

Think of container gardens as small, portable gardens. They are fun, quick, easy to create, and require little space. Container gardens bring color to decks, porches, or patios. Pots are terrific for filling in color in a garden where needed; just place them in any gap.

Purchase a good quality potting mix; most are soil-less mixes and benefit from the addition of about 10 percent compost. It is also wise to mix in some time-release fertilizer and water-retention polymer beads or hydrogel; both are available at the nursery. Follow package instructions; be sure to keep the hydrogel 4" under the surface of the pot to avoid wicking water out of the plant. Soil-less mixes are good for hanging pots as they weigh less than richer mixes.

A typical design for a container would be a tall plant in the center or back of the container, midsize plants surrounding it, delicate or frilly plants for filler, and vines or plants that drape

---

SOME FAVORITE ANNUALS

AGERATUM (*Ageratum* spp.)—varieties 6" to 24" tall, powder-puff blue flowers, full sun

CALIFORNIA POPPIES (*Eschscholzia californica*)—10" to 16" tall, bright and pastel colors, full sun

COSMOS (*Cosmos bipinnatus*)—4' to 6' tall, fast grower; single, double, bright and pastel flowers, sun

DATURA (*Datura metel*)—3' to 5' tall; large fragrant trumpet flowers, white plus color hybrids, poisonous, sun

DIANTHUS (*Dianthus* spp.)—6" to 24" tall, fragrant carnation flowers, many colors, sun

IMPATIENS (*Impatiens* spp.)—1' to 2' tall, many flower colors, shade

SNAPDRAGON (*Antirrhinum majus*)—6" to 30" tall, fast; many bright colors, fun for kids, sun

SUNFLOWER (*Helianthus* spp.)—2' to 15' tall, mostly bright colors, edible seeds, fun for kids, sun

ZINNIA (*Zinnia elegans*)—6" to 36" tall, many colors, cutting, sun

The mix of roses, lavender, yarrow, daisies, and coreopsis in this sunny border is a cornucopia of color and textures.

over the sides. Plan colors, textures, and bloom times as you would any flower border. Mistakes can easily be corrected. You can also create a container for a single season then, for a different look, change plants to ones that flower later in the year.

Before planting, move the container to where you intend to keep it during the season. It is much easier to move around before it is filled with soil, plants, and water. Fill the container to within about 3" of the surface, then mix in the hydrogel and slow-release fertilizers. Then start planting from the center out or back to front. Continue to add plants by decreasing height and size, finally adding the vines or plants that weep over the sides of the container. Then water thoroughly. A few days later, or later in the season, add more plants as required. Remember that plants in your container should be planted no deeper than they were in the nursery pot; thus the top of the plant remains at the same level.

Container gardens dry out very rapidly and thus require regular watering. You also should fertilize every couple of weeks, despite the time-release fertilizer in the mix. Some plants, like petunias, can be fertilized with every watering. This will help promote vigorous growth and flowering. If growth is too energetic, cut plants back to maintain an attractive overall appearance.

Consider theme container plantings for fun. Try a desert theme (cacti and succulents); fragrance garden (heliotrope, pineapple mint, and nicotiana); mini herb garden (basil, chives, and mint); pizza garden (tomatoes, oregano, and peppers); salad garden (leaf lettuce and cherry tomatoes); or Simon-and-Garfunkel theme (parsley, sage, rosemary, and thyme).

Crocuses and other bulbs give an early-season infusion of color.

For a container, you can use almost anything that will hold soil, not fall apart when wet, and be portable. Most people use large plastic pots, which do not dry out as fast as porous clay pots and weigh and cost much less. Many are now designed to resemble expensive and decorative clay pots. Whiskey barrels, galvanized tubs, wicker baskets, ice cream buckets, old boots, and anything else you can dream up or find at a garage sale also work. Small containers can be fun, even if only temporary, to house just a single plant.

Large containers are a bit easier to work with and will dry out more slowly between waterings. Perhaps the largest containers I have seen were cars, pickup truck beds, and boats turned into planters. The smallest planter I have seen was a demitasse cup.

BULBS

Many of the most familiar plants grow from bulbs. There are several different fleshy underground storage types, including corms, tubers, and rhizomes, which are handled in very much the same ways as bulbs. A bulb merchant will sell all types. Daffodils, lilies, chives, snowdrops, tulips, and hyacinths all require similar handling. They are among the easiest of all plants to grow and enjoy in your garden; you should plant many of them. You can also interplant bulbs in flowerbeds and incorporate some into containers. One terrific combination is a bed of lilies, daffodils, and daylilies. This will give you a long season of color with very little work.

Most bulbs are planted in the fall at a depth of about three times the height of the bulb. The bulb package has instructions on it, including a diagram to show the root end, which is planted downward. You can plant one bulb at a time with a trowel or hundreds in an area where you have cut and rolled back the grass. If you plant a large quantity of bulbs of the same type in one area, a single color of one hybrid looks the best. For a formal look, plant bulbs in a straight line, soldier style. For a natural look, scatter bulbs by tossing them onto a prepared bed, then plant them where they land. Fertilize bulbs with an appropriate fertilizer when planting, then again in the spring and fall of most years. Allow the foliage of the bulbs to yellow and die naturally without doing anything to them; cut and remove the foliage after it has become brown.

All of the bulbs mentioned will persist for years in the garden if planted deep enough, except the tulips, which decline after the first year and should be replaced after two years. Beginning gardeners should stick with these hardy bulbs as opposed to dahlias, which are beautiful, but which have corms that need to be dug up and stored inside each winter. Select only a few bulbs or plants each year that require such special efforts, and always buy more bulbs than you think you will need. Bulbs produce so much color and excitement early in the year that they are one of the best investments you can make. They are low-maintenance gardening at its best.

GROUND COVERS

Ground covers, which are low-growing plants used as grass alternatives, are practical and can be a design feature too. Landscape architects, in their design plans, may only use six or so plants in a large area. This unity of design creates strong visual impact. You can mimic that idea in all or parts of your landscape. Imagine a section of your garden with five to seven small trees, perhaps the heritage birch, underplanted with nothing but bishop's hat, Russian cypress, or spurge, or any number of other combinations of woody plants and ground cover. This type of design makes a quiet, contemplative space that is also low maintenance.

You can alter the appearance of lawns by planting ground covers in place of grass. Well-grown grass is very uniform, with little textural and light-to-dark variation; ground covers offer a variety of visual interest. However, most ground covers will not endure much foot traffic, one of the great assets of the traditional lawn. Use ground covers where you will walk little and select plants that will accept more traffic than others. Visualize a full-sun area that dries out rapidly, where it is a challenge to grow attractive grass. As an alternative, plant succulents close together, say stonecrop (*Sedum*) or hen and chicks (*Sempervivum*). They come in a wide variety of foliage colors—gray, black, silver, and red—and will make an attractive alternative.

Ground covers can also be wisely used on a slope that is hard and dangerous to mow and will help prevent erosion of that steep slope. The cut-leafed lace shrub (*Stephanandra incisa* 'Crispa') grows well in challenging locations and will hold the soil in place.

The biggest selling point for ground covers over grass is their practicality; they save work and natural resources. Grass is a high-maintenance plant that requires regular care, feeding, and watering. A carefully selected and planted bed of ground covers will look good and perform well without all that fuss.

Like all plants, ground covers perform best in well-prepared soil that is suited to them. Plant moisture-loving plants in water-retentive, organic soil, and succulents and herbs in well-drained, lean soil. Know the needs of the plants you select and prepare the area accordingly.

Many books and plant tags will give the mature size of plants; ground cover plants may be labeled with planting density information. For determining how many plants we need, we are most concerned with how much each plant spreads. We eventually want plants to completely cover the soil to prevent the sun from germinating weed seeds. Measure the area and calculate the square footage you will be planting. For example, imagine a bed that is about 10' by 10', which is 100 square feet. If one plant of the potential ground cover spreads to 1' by 1', you will need 100 plants to cover the area. If an individual plant covers 18" by 18", how many will you need? If you plant a row across the front of a border that is 10' long, or 120", it will take about six plants to fill in that row. In our border, the depth is also 10', so it will take a row of six plants to cover a single row in that direction. You have six rows needing six plants, so you need at least 36 plants. It's always best to buy a few more than you calculate you need.

For better coverage, stagger plants in a tic-tac-toe pattern. Often when the initial planting is finished, you will have bare ground between plants. You should cover this open space with a minimum of 3" of organic mulch. This will break down over time and enrich the soil, keep weeds to a minimum, and help keep the soil moist. Continue to add mulch in future years until the plantings are mature; fertilize each spring. Another choice would be to fill in with annuals until the ground covers have time to grow and spread.

Some favorite ground covers for shade include bedstraw, bishop's hat, carpet bugle, foamflower, hosta, lily-of-the-valley, spurge, sweet box, wild ginger, wintergreen, and vinca. Ground covers for sun include bramble, creeping jenny (or moneywort), heath, juniper, plumbago, Russian cypress, and scotch heather.

DESIGN FOR PRIVACY

In medieval times, an enclosed garden provided security and seclusion from marauding invaders. Today, we have neighbors and others whom we need to keep at a distance at least some of the time. We also live in a time of shrinking lot size, so we do not have acres separating us from others. In an urban area, the problem is likely to be worse than in a rural location.

Some views may be protected, and most municipalities have standards for fencing, some for front yard vegetation. You will need to consider local laws, regulations, and restrictions as you create a plan for privacy in your garden. It is critical to know where property lines are. Remember that when erecting fences or planting, anything placed on the line belongs to both you and your neighbors. If you are considering planting trees or shrubs that will eventually grow over the property line, it is best to discuss this with your neighbors first.

Start by identifying what you need to block out and what you want to preserve. In design, we talk of the "borrowed view"—some area or feature not on our property we want to continue to see or even incorporate into our plans. A view of a park, natural water feature, or rock outcropping on the adjoining property can add much to your landscape plan.

Also think about which views you want to cover up, such as an unsightly garage or car up on cement blocks. You can carefully place a single tree, or a group of trees, to block out a problem view. If the problem is year round, then consider evergreen trees or shrubs. Planting a hedge, a mixed shrub and tree border with deciduous and evergreens, a single well-placed tree, or constructing berms, fences, or a tall wall fountain works as well for a city lot as for a larger property where you create garden rooms.

Hedges take up the least space but are often labor intensive. The formal, carved lines take constant trimming. An informal hedge with mixed shrubs and trees will take more space but will require much less work. You can also plant a series of upright growing columnar-shaped trees so that at maturity the growing tips touch or mesh.

Berms are artificial mounds of soil often created to solve problems, for example, to help cut traffic noise. You can use soil from another spot on your property or purchase a load of topsoil for the project. Never build small berms; they look like mistakes. They should be a minimum of 2½' tall and 4' wide. Maintain a similar proportion for larger berms. You can add much more height to garden areas by planting on berms.

When building a fence, you should keep in mind the style and materials of your house and the area. Stone fences look great in New England; adobe is at home in the Southwest. Fences can be softened by planting shrubs in front of them or adding climbing vines. The vines can be on a trellis just in front of the fence to give you more height for privacy.

■ Plants for Success

PERENNIALS

NEW ENGLAND ASTER
Aster novae-angliae 'Alma Potschke'
Category: fall flowering perennial
Use: in mixed borders
Soil: well-drained, moderate fertility
Hardiness: zones 4 to 8
Mature size: 3' tall by 2' wide

New England asters are a robust addition to any fall garden—big, beautiful, and bountiful. They produce lots of daisy-type flowers (one common name is Michaelmas daisy) on tough, almost woody 3' stems. Over a six-week time period, 'Alma Potschke' produces magenta-pink flowers

---

Aster hybrid (*Aster* x *frikartii* 'Jungfrau')

that blend well with a wide range of other plants, including coneflowers, 'Autumn Joy' stonecrop, and grasses shifting into autumn colors.

New England asters thrive in a variety of conditions but do best in full sun in decent well-drained soil. They perform well with moist soils during active growth. Plant them from containers in spring or fall and allow adequate room as they are strong growers. To reinvigorate and keep control of the plants, divide them every two years. Cut back or shear your plants around July 4 in New England. Fertilize plants when growth resumes in spring. It is also best to allow air circulation around plants to prevent powdery mildew, although New England asters are more resistant than most asters. Too little moisture during growth can also weaken the plants and leave them susceptible to disease.

Other asters to consider: *Aster novae-angliae* 'Harrington's Pink'—about 3' to 4' tall, clear pink flowers, needs division less frequently than many; *Aster novi-belgii* 'Marie Ballard'—about 4' tall, double powder blue flowers; *Aster* x *frikartii* 'Mönch'—2' tall by 3' wide, soft lavender blue blooms in late summer.

Potential problems: powdery mildew, few pests.

LADY'S MANTLE
Alchemilla mollis
Category: sun-loving perennial
Use: massed in edge paths, borders, and herb gardens or alone in container
Soil: well-drained but moist
Hardiness: zones 3 to 9
Mature size: 1' to 2' tall by 18" wide

Lady's mantle is an old-fashioned, dependable, and attractive plant in the garden. The rounded gray-green leaves, up to 6" wide, have a wavy or scalloped edge, and the plants are covered with clouds of chartreuse flowers in mid- to late spring. The hair that covers the leaves makes them soft to the touch and able to hold drops of water, engendering the common name "lady's mantle."

Plant lady's mantle in full sun in well-drained soil that retains some moisture; plants need little maintenance or dividing. Space 3" tall plants 8" apart for ground cover in a large area, but allow no foot traffic. In the unusual case that they start to look bad in midsummer, cut them back; maintain with a lawn mower set at 3" height. Use lady's mantle in mixed borders or edges, along brick paths, and in containers and herb gardens. For a relaxed look, let the plant spill over the edge of hardscape or containers. Remove old flowers to promote a second bloom. Cut flowers can be used fresh in arrangements or dried. Lady's mantle may self-sow in some gardens, but is rarely a problem; just move the seedlings to another section of the garden or give them to friends.

Potential problems: winter wet conditions can kill the plants, but few pests or diseases attack lady's mantle.

Lady's mantle (*Alchemilla mollis*)

FALSE INDIGO
Baptisia australis
Category: sun-loving perennial
Use: in mixed borders
Soil: well-drained, organic
Hardiness: zones 3 to 10
Mature size: 3' to 5' tall by 3' wide

False indigo is a handsome native perennial that produces many spikes of indigo blue flowers in early summer. The attractive gray-green foliage appears early in spring and is an asset throughout the growing season. After flowering, large pea pod–shaped seedheads form, which can be left on the plants or cut and used in arrangements. These pods will last until late fall; some people even like the browned pods through winter. As the seeds ripen, the pods will rattle when you shake them like a wand; kids love this game. If you desire to grow more plants from seed, scrape the seed lightly with sandpaper or a file before planting to encourage germination.

Plant container-grown false indigo in the spring. It is adaptable to less-perfect growing conditions but will do best in full sun and deep, organic soil with plenty of moisture during active growth. At full height and in flower, the plant will lean over or "flop"; if you don't like this look, you may want to stake the plants. In shady locations, the plant will stretch a bit taller, flop more, and produce fewer flowers. The plant spreads at a reasonable but not invasive pace via underground runners. Give it room to expand or remove new lateral growth occasionally and give it to a friend or plant it in another location in your garden. The indigo blue flowers and gray-green foliage blend with almost any plant. Another false indigo to consider is *Baptisia leucantha*, which has white flowers on plants about 4' tall and 2' wide.

Potential problems: no major pests or diseases.

FOXGLOVE
Digitalis purpurea
Category: shade biennial/perennial
Use: in mixed borders; cottage, formal, and woodland gardens
Soil: well-drained, rich, organic
Hardiness: zones 4 to 8
Mature size: 2' to 4' tall by 1½' wide

The old-fashioned and dependable foxglove makes its presence felt in the early summer garden with a lavish display of flowers. Digitalis is the famous medicinal plant used to prevent heart failure, so it is considered poisonous. Removing spent flowers will prolong bloom, but leave some seedpods to spread about the garden in order to ensure a continuing supply of foxglove in future years. Foxglove is technically a biennial, which flowers in the second year, sets seed, and then dies, but some persists and new seedlings pop up with such abandon there are serendipitous flowers throughout your garden. The upright stems, full of hanging trumpet flowers, often

ABOVE: False indigo (*Baptisia australis*)
BELOW: Foxglove (*Digitalis purpurea*)

Purple coneflower (*Echinacea purpurea*)

with dramatic markings in the throat, produce vertical interest anywhere they are planted, whether in a formal border or more relaxed mixed borders, cottage gardens, or woodland gardens.

Plant container-grown plants in spring into moist, organic, acidic, and well-drained soils; keep moist during active growth. Foxglove can handle lots of sun in northern New England, although it is considered a shade plant. To spread plants for future years, cut off a stem of dried seedpods and use it like a magic wand to sprinkle seeds throughout the garden.

More foxgloves to consider: 'Foxy'—3' tall plants in rose, yellow, and white; 'Excelsior Hybrids'—5' tall with mauve, pink, rose, white, and yellow flowers; 'Giant Shirley'—5' tall with 3' spikes of dark and light pink flowers.

Potential problems: aphids, mealy bugs, and Japanese beetles; powdery mildew in areas with poor air circulation.

PURPLE CONEFLOWER
Echinacea purpurea
Category: sun-loving perennial
Use: in mixed borders, meadows, or butterfly gardens
Soil: well-drained
Hardiness: zones 3 to 10
Mature size: 3' tall by 1 ½' wide

This well-known, low-maintenance perennial produces attractive purple-petalled flowers with a dark "nose" in the center; the petals droop a bit, producing the "cone" of the common name. Echinacea is also a legendary herbal remedy that strengthens the immune system, although you should avoid experimenting with home potions.

This eastern and central U.S. native plant will grow well any place with decent garden soil and reasonable drainage; it does best in full sun, although it is adaptable to less ideal conditions. Plant it at the same soil depth as it comes in its original container and water it well until established; it will be very drought tolerant after that. Coneflowers can be used in mixed borders, planted alone, or massed for dramatic effect. They have a long blooming season from summer into fall; remove old flowers to prolong flowering. Some gardeners allow the dry stems and noses to remain after flowering to supply some winter structure in the garden and food for birds. Mature plants can be left undisturbed for years.

Other echinaceas: 'Magnus'—deep lavender pink flowers are flatter and a bit larger, approaching 4" in diameter; 'White Swan'—the creamy white version of the purple coneflower is somewhat fragrant and grows up to 4' tall; 'Kim's Knee High'—this dwarf coneflower is only 18" to 24" in height and useful in front of borders; 'Art's Pride' (trademarked as Orange Meadowbrite)—orange-tangerine flowers bloom June into July and sporadically into September.

Potential problems: mildew, Japanese beetles; soggy soil or winter wet conditions are deadly.

DAYLILY
Hemerocallis spp.
Category: perennial
Use: in mixed borders or massed as edging
Soil: well-drained, organic
Hardiness: zones 3 to 9
Mature size: 1' to 4' tall

Daylilies are high-performance plants, easy to grow under almost any conditions. Individual trumpet-shaped flowers last only one day, but plants continuously produce new ones during the flowering season. Whole stalks can be cut for arrangements. Flowers may be red, orange, pink, purple, yellow, white, or multicolor. Organically grown flowers are edible; harvest at the tight bud stage and sauté in oil. They make an interesting, nutty-tasting side dish.

Treat daylilies well by planting them in the sun in good, well-drained, organic soil with adequate moisture, and they will reward you with terrific performance and numerous flowers. They do well even in less perfect conditions, although they produce fewer blooms. Interplant early and late bloomers for continuous bloom throughout the season; add early-flowering narcissus and late-flowering lilies for a full season of bloom.

Plant daylilies in spring or fall from container or bare-root plants (or divisions from a friend's garden). The bare roots look very beat up, almost dead, but do not worry; they will revive and thrive once planted. Set the crown of the plant just below the soil surface. Water well until established; afterward daylilies have low moisture requirements and are drought tolerant. Fertilize at half the strength suggested on the label of a flowering plant fertilizer. Mulch plants with an organic material.

Other daylilies to consider: 'Happy Returns'—soft lemon-yellow flowers, 18" tall; 'Hyperion'—fragrant lemon-yellow 5" flowers blooming midseason; 'Stella d'Oro'—yellow flowers, slight fragrance, rebloomer spring to fall, 1' to 2' tall plants.

Potential problems: few diseases or pests except deer.

PLANTAIN LILY
Hosta 'Golden Tiara'
Category: shade perennial
Use: as edging, ground cover
Soil: moist, organic
Hardiness: zones 3 to 9
Mature size: 12" tall by 16" wide

Hostas are terrific plants for virtually any shady spot in the garden when there is sufficient moisture to promote good growth. From spring until frost, they put on a good show of foliage with a burst of flowering. *Hosta* 'Golden Tiara' is a quick-spreading and attractive little hosta. Most leaves are about 3" wide by 4" long on plants that grow into a mound about 12" high,

ABOVE: Daylily (*Hemerocallis* 'Stella d'Oro')
BELOW: Plantain lily (*Hosta* 'Golden Tiara')

Blazing star (*Liatris spicata* 'Kolbold')

with a spread to 16". The leaves are light green with a muted yellow margin. A few small plants can cover an area in several years. There are purple flowers in midsummer, but the main reason to grow 'Golden Tiara' is the fast-spreading foliage.

Plant 'Golden Tiara' in a light shade location, although it will take full shade or part sun, with lots of organic matter in the soil. Maintain the planting depth of the plant in the pot when you move it into the landscape. Water well, mulch with organic matter, and keep well watered until the plant is established (one to two years). Mature plants can be divided in the spring or left undisturbed for years. They will die to the ground after a hard frost. Clean up the debris prior to winter.

Other hostas to consider are: 'Blue Moon'—small blue leaves about 2" wide and 3" long; plant grows into a clump 5" high and 9" wide; late summer white flowers; leaves are pest-resistant. 'Frances Williams'—8" wide by 10" long medium blue-green puckered leaves with yellow edges; plant grows slowly into impressive mound 32" high and 40" wide. *H. sieboldiana*—12" wide and 14" long deep-veined blue-green leaves; plant grows into mound 30" tall and 52" wide in about five years; white flowers in early summer.

Potential problems: slugs, snails, and deer.

BLAZING STAR
Liatris spicata 'Kobold'
Category: upright summer perennial
Use: in mixed borders, meadows, butterfly gardens
Soil: sandy to moderately fertile, well-drained
Hardiness: zones 3 to 10
Mature size: 2' to 3' tall by 2' wide

Blazing star is a terrific, easy, and long-lived perennial that blooms from summer into fall. 'Kobold' is a dark purple color selection of an American native and is very adaptable to reasonable growing conditions (somewhat fertile well-drained soil that receives full sun). The flowers open from the top of the spike down so you can trim off the faded areas as desired and still have attractive structural and color interest in your garden. The plants are very drought resistant once established.

Plant the bare-root tuberous root stock or container plants in well-drained and moderately fertile soil in full sun in the spring. The plants can withstand some shade and sandy soil. Blazing star can be used in a mixed border, meadow, butterfly or wild garden, and is exceptional in a vase, whether fresh or dried. The upright spikes of dark purple flowers are an effective design element in formal or natural gardens. They combine well with ornamental grasses or with 2' tall blue fescue (*Festuca ovina glauca*), with its silver blue spiky leaves, or 3' to 6' tall blue switch grass 'Heavy Metal' (*Panicum virgatum*) with its silver blue-green leaves.

Other blazing stars to consider: 'August Glory'—3' to 4' tall with purple-blue flowers; 'Floristan White'—3' tall with white flowers; *L. pycnostachya*—4' to 5' tall with purple flowers (stake or use in meadow, mulch in cold areas).

Potential problems: few pests or diseases.

CHRYSANTHEMUM 'BECKY'
Leucanthemum x superbum 'Becky'
Category: summer perennial
Use: in mixed borders, cottage gardens
Soil: fertile, well-drained
Hardiness: zones 4 to 9
Mature size: 3' tall by 1½' wide

Becky' is a showy, long-flowering perennial (June or July into September with deadheading) that produces white daisy-like blooms with yellow centers. It is indispensable in gardens because of its long bloom and sturdy dark shiny foliage that is evergreen in warm areas. 'Becky' is terrific in combination with lemon-yellow flowers, works to pull together pink and blue flowers, and blends with virtually any other flowering plant. It looks particularly good with blue flowers of Russian sage (*Perovskia atriplicifolia*) or the bright red flowers of falling stars (*Crocosmia* 'Lucifer'), and is especially useful in sunny borders, mixed plantings, or in large masses.

Plant container-grown plants about 2' apart in good, well-drained garden soil in spring. Fertilize throughout the growing season. In cold areas, mulch plants after frost. Avoid overhead watering for best appearance. 'Becky' requires little maintenance; divide in spring or after flowering. This chrysanthemum was the Perennial Plant Association's Plant of the Year in 2003.

Other mums: 'Aglaya'—frilly double flowers on 1½' to 2' tall plants; 'Alaska'—single 2" flowers on 2' to 3' tall plants (cut back after first flowering for second flowering); 'Little Princess'—large flowers on very compact plants (up to 1' tall); 'Starburst'—large 6" flowers early in season on 3' tall plants.

Potential problems: winter wet areas decrease survival or cause verticillium wilt; plants are pest resistant except for aphids.

RUSSIAN SAGE
Perovskia atriplicifolia 'Blue Spire'
Category: sun-loving perennial
Use: massed or as accent plant
Soil: well-drained, average fertility
Hardiness: zones 5 to 10
Mature size: 4' tall by 18" wide

This silvery gem makes a terrific addition to any sunny location that is well drained. It is not edible but is very aromatic, and has a cloud of purple-blue flowers that seem to float above the stems in the last two months of summer. Silver stems and light green leaves have silver-gray hairs on them. The variety 'Blue Spire' has fernlike leaves that are quite decorative. 'Blue Haze' has nearly smooth-edged leaves and paler blue flowers. There is some name confusion in the trade, so pick out the varieties of this plant you like best at the nursery.

Small Russian sage plants need a little extra care and adequate water to get them growing; once established, the plants will survive well on very little water and care. They are vigorous

ABOVE: Chrysanthemum 'Becky' (*Leucanthemum* x *superbum* 'Becky')
BELOW: Russian sage (*Perovskia atriplicifolia* 'Blue Spire')

growers; leave stems standing over the winter for some structure and interest, then cut back to the ground in spring. Even at around 4' tall, Russian sage's open construction makes it possible to place anywhere, including the front of a border. It works well as an accent plant or massed with other silver and gray plants or contrasted with reddish-leaved barberries or dark-green foliage plants. It is also often paired with succulent sedums, which require similar growing conditions. Plant a number of plants close together, say 9" apart, for a denser effect.

Potential problems: soggy soil will kill this plant; use rapidly draining soil.

LAMB'S EARS
Stachys byzantina 'Helene von Stein'
Category: sun-loving perennial
Use: as edging, ground cover
Soil: well-drained
Hardiness: zones 4 to 10
Mature size: 8" high

Helene von Stein' lamb's ears (occasionally called 'Countess Helene von Stein' or 'Big Ears'—we seem to have so little respect for royalty) has leaves about twice as large as the standard lamb's ears. This species of lamb's ears has fuzzy silvery-white leaves about 6" long by 2" wide, sure to delight children. It makes a good-sized edging plant; let it sprawl and it will soften the edges of stone or cement walkways. It also provides a dramatic ground cover, although it will not endure foot traffic; space plants about 24" apart for this use. You can use it in an herb garden, moon garden, or containers.

Plant from containers in spring or fall in well-drained soil in sunny or part-sun locations. Every few years a flower will appear; simply remove it if you do not like it, as many gardeners do. 'Silver Carpet' is a nonflowering and less vigorous form of regular-sized lamb's ears, but 'Countess' seems to take more heat and humidity than the other varieties. All silver-leaved lamb's ears are usable in harsh seashore conditions; you could kill them with kindness with too-rich soil or too much water. They may need dividing after five years; otherwise, they are extremely low-maintenance plants.

In addition to the cultivars described above, you may want to consider the species plant, *Stachys byzantina*, with leaves about 3" to 4" long by 1 ½" wide and small pink flowers early in summer (some gardeners remove them). Plants will reach about 18" high if flowers remain; space them about 18" apart.

Potential problems: very deer and pest resistant.

Lamb's ears (*Stachys byzantina*)

ABOVE: Butterfly bush (*Buddleia davidii* 'Black Knight')
BELOW: Summersweet (*Clethra alnifolia*)

SHRUBS

BUTTERFLY BUSH
Buddleia davidii
Category: flowering shrub
Use: in mixed borders, butterfly gardens
Soil: well-drained, fertile
Hardiness: zones 5 to 9
Mature size: 8' to 10' tall by about 5' wide (occasionally 15' by 10')

The butterfly bush is a very adaptable plant that produces lilac-shaped clusters of fragrant flowers. It is available in many different colors, all of which attract lots of butterflies to your garden. It can die back to the ground in the North; in all areas, cut plants back to within 6" of the ground in early spring. This will keep plants in better shape and produce more flowers as it only flowers on new wood, new stems, or branches of the current growing season.

Butterfly bush does best in full sun in well-drained fertile soils, but adapts to lean or sandy soils in part-sun locations; water well to establish growth. New, vigorous growth produces the most and largest flowers, which are useful as cut flowers although not particularly long-lived. Virtually all selections are vigorous growing plants. The 'Nanho' types grow only to about 3' to 5' tall and are more suited for confined areas or containers.

Some choices include: 'Black Knight'—cold tolerant with very dark purple flowers; 'Fascination'—extra long strong grower to 15" or more; 'Harlequin'—a less vigorous variegated grower with cream-edged leaves and red-purple flowers; 'Nanho Alba'—a spreader with white flowers and slender leaves; 'Nanho Blue'—mauve-blue flowers with gray-green foliage; 'Nanho Purple'—purple flowers with silver-green foliage; 'White Bouquet'—8" long white flowers.

Potential problems: rarely bothered by pests and diseases.

SUMMERSWEET
Clethra alnifolia
Category: fragrant native shrub
Use: in mixed borders, woodland gardens, and seashore locations
Soil: moist, acid
Hardiness: zones 3 to 9
Mature size: 8' tall by 8' wide

Summersweet is a midsized, dense multistemmed shrub that grows to 8' tall with a spread of 8', although it can be kept smaller by pruning. This native plant spreads by suckering; to control, use a spade to cut its runners and remove any undesired new growth. A profusion of fragrant white bottlebrush flowers appear in late summer. Rich dark green foliage turns an attractive yellow color in fall.

Summersweet handles full sun in northern states, although it does best in partial shade in soils with adequate moisture. It does well in a wide range of conditions and is very drought tolerant once established. It is useful in shade gardens, seashore plantings, massed, or as a complement to perennials in a mixed border. Plant container-grown specimens in spring into rich, organic-based acidic soil and keep well watered until established. In very cold climates and very wet soil, plant it a couple of inches above the level grown in the container; mulch in winter.

Other summersweet to consider: 'Compacta'—the Long Island Gold Medal Award Plant, a slow-growing form to 5' tall with spread to 6'; 'Hummingbird'—a dwarf form to 2' to 3' high and bit wider with glossy foliage; 'Ruby Spice'—dark pink–flowered form to 6' tall and equally wide.

Potential problems: deer rarely eat or damage them and they have few other pests and diseases.

DWARF FOTHERGILLA
Fothergilla gardenii
Category: fragrant native shrub
Uses: in mixed borders, woodland and natural gardens, along foundations
Soil: moist, well-drained, acidic
Hardiness: zones 5 to 8
Mature size: 3' to 4' tall by 3' wide

Dwarf fothergilla is native to the southeastern United States and has been grown in American gardens for over 200 years. George Washington grew it in his garden. It grows in sunny, wet habitats, and attains a height of 3' to 4', occasionally to 6', which can easily be accommodated in small gardens. In late April to early May, it produces beautiful white fragrant bottlebrush flowers about 2" long and 1" in diameter. It will survive in the shade, although a plant that receives at least a half-day of sun will produce more flowers and will grow in a more round and compact habit. The outstanding fall foliage color is a brilliant yellow to orange or scarlet, sometimes all mixed together. Fall color varies by individual plant and is also related to how much sun it receives; more sun equals better fall color. The species has much better fall color than newer, more recently named selections.

This multistem plant, which requires no pruning other than damaged branches, can be utilized in a woodland situation, a mixed border, a natural garden, a mass planting, as a part of a foundation planting, or in front of an evergreen border. Plant container-grown fothergillas in spring or in moist, well-drained acidic soil in fall. The dwarf fothergilla is a selection of the Long Island Gold Medal Plant Award.

Potential problems: relatively pest- and disease-free.

Dwarf fothergilla (*Fothergilla gardenii*)

ABOVE: Oak leaf hydrangea (*Hydrangea quercifolia*)
BELOW: Mountain laurel (*Kalmia latifolia*)

OAK-LEAF HYDRANGEA
Hydrangea quercifolia
Category: summer flowering shrub
Use: in mixed borders, along edge of woodland
Soil: well-drained, somewhat fertile
Hardiness: zones 4 to 8
Mature size: 6' tall by 6' wide (occasionally to 8')

This hydrangea provides decorative accents to any landscape with its interesting oak leaf–shaped foliage and profusion of large, up to 12" long white cone-shaped flowers. It performs best in full sun and will produce the most flowers and good fall color farther north; although it will take light shade in more southern areas.

Plant oak-leaf hydrangea in spring or fall in well-drained soil with reasonable fertility. Fertilize in spring when growth resumes. The flowers will dry on the plant and provide decorative interest in the fall and winter garden. This hydrangea's growth habit is a bit loose or coarse and some people prefer it planted in more naturalistic settings, although it seems an attractive specimen plant to many. Plants three years old and older have cinnamon-colored peeling bark for winter interest. This species was selected as a winner of the Long Island Gold Medal Plant Award.

Varieties of oak-leaf hydrangea to consider: 'Alice'—compact form with white flowers turning pink as they mature; 'Pee Wee'—one of smallest forms (to only 3') with full-sized flowers blooming midsummer and excellent burgundy fall foliage; 'Snow Flake'—attractive double-flowered appearance; 'Snow Queen'—smaller growing to 5' tall, white upright flowers turning pink as they mature.

Potential problems: protect young plants in winter in zones 4 and 5; mulch in all zones to keep the rootzone cool.

MOUNTAIN LAUREL
Kalmia latifolia
Category: flowering broadleaf evergreen
Use: for shady borders, naturalizing effect
Soil: moist, acidic
Hardiness: zones 4 to 9
Mature size: 4' to 8' tall, not quite as wide

Mountain laurel is a beautiful native plant with attractive, dark green, glossy foliage that works hard in the cultivated garden. In late spring or early summer it begins with dark-colored buds that explode with masses of 1" bell-shaped flowers. Individual flowers usually have decorative spots of contrasting color in the throat.

In its native habitat, you find mountain laurel in forest shade, but it is highly adaptable to a sunny location if you provide even moisture and keep the roots cool by mulching. It can be planted alone or massed in mixed or naturalized settings as a shade border. Plant in acidic soil in spring or fall from container-grown plants and mulch with organic matter (shredded hardwood leaves or bark chips); keep well watered until plants are established. Mountain laurel can be combined with other acid-loving plants like rhododendrons, azaleas, and hollies. This species and its cultivars are amenable to pruning, which is best done immediately after flowers fade, as flowers are produced on new growth of wood.

Some varieties of mountain laurel include: 'Alba'—pure white flowers; 'Carousel'—lavender buds open to intricate purple-cinnamon starburst pattern; 'Freckles'—pink buds open to cream-white flower with ten purple spots in throat; 'Pink Charm'—deep pink buds open to rich pink flowers; 'Snowdrift'—compact to 5' tall with pure white flowers and glossy green foliage.

JAPANESE PIERIS (not andromeda)
Pieris japonica
Category: winter-flowering broadleaf evergreen
Use: in mixed borders
Soil: well-drained, organic, moist
Hardiness: zones 4 to 8
Mature size: from 6' to 9' tall

Japanese pieris is an attractive, neat-growing, upright broadleaf evergreen shrub available in a wide range of color choices. The buds are attractive all winter. In the early spring, sometimes March, the cream-colored fragrant flowers hang down in bunches like pearls grouped on a number of strings. The attractive glossy green foliage looks good throughout the year.

This is a slow-growing shrub that is worth the investment in time and patience. You can easily combine it with other broadleaf evergreens or acid-loving plants such as rhododendrons, azaleas, and hollies, although pieris is not as fussy about the pH as the others. You can also use it as an accent plant in a fern garden, in a mixed border, or in a woodland garden.

Plant pieris in spring or fall in well-drained soils, supplemented with organic matter, that retain moisture during the growing season but do not remain wet during winter. A location in the sun or part sun will produce the most flowers and best growth, although pieris can handle some shade.

Some varieties of pieris include: 'Dorothy Wycoff—compact, to 5', vigorous grower, dark red flower buds opening into white flowers; 'Mountain Fire'—to 6', new growth opens brilliant red.

Potential problems: give winter cold protection in zones 4 and 5; lace bug can be a problem in some parts of New England.

Japanese pieris (*Pieris japonica*)

ABOVE: Burkwood's viburnum (*Viburnum* x *burkwoodii*)
BELOW: Meidiland rose (*Rosa* 'Bonica')

BURKWOOD'S VIBURNUM
Viburnum x *burkwoodii*
Category: fragrant shrub
Use: in mixed borders
Soil: moist, fertile, well-drained
Hardiness: zones 4 to 8
Mature size: 8' to 10' tall by about 6' wide

Burkwood's viburnum is one of the toughest of this clan of wonderful landscape shrubs. It will withstand much cold and reward gardeners with attractive pink buds opening to very fragrant white waxy flowers in snowball shapes in late spring. Fully deciduous in the North, the leaves are an attractive glossy dark green with brown-gray undersides and show up well against any dark background of evergreens. This kind of background obscures its somewhat ungainly growth habit, which might require some pruning.

Plant Burkwood's viburnum in spring or fall from container or balled-and-burlapped specimens; always remove burlap, wires, and twine when planting. Select a planting location in the full sun or part sun that has moist, fertile well-drained soil. More shade will cause the plant to stretch and produce fewer flowers.

Other viburnums to consider are: *V.* x *carlcephalum*—vigorous growth to 8' tall, fragrant round white flowers in May; *V. carlesii*—upright and wide growth to 8', very fragrant light pink or white flowers, red fruit in August, red fall foliage in most years; *V. plicatum* var. *tomentosum*—double-file form to 12' tall with horizontal tiers of flowers; *V. plicatum* var. *tomentosum* 'Mariesii'—dark red flower buds persist for weeks on 7' tall plants, then bring clove-scented flowers.

Potential problems: free of most pests and diseases (all varieties listed above are resistant to the viburnum leaf beetle).

Roses

MEIDILAND ROSE
Rosa 'Bonica'
Category: shrub rose
Use: in mixed borders and hedges, along foundations
Soil: fertile, well-drained
Hardiness: zones 4 to 9
Mature size: about 4' tall, 4' wide

The Bonica shrub rose in the French-developed Meidiland group is one of the best roses known for its high degree of pest and disease tolerance. It is substantially easier to grow than typical tea roses. Bonicas flower profusely over a long season with 2 ½" petal-rich double candy-pink flowers. There are up to five flowers clustered on each 4' arching cane. The good, midgreen foliage holds up well throughout the season. Bonica works well in a mixed border, massed, in a foundation planting, or as a colorful hedge. This rose was an All-American award winner in 1987 and the World's Favorite Rose in 1997 according to the World Federation of Rose Societies.

Plant container-grown Bonicas in the spring or fall in fertile, well-drained soil. Plants appreciate an organic mulch about 2" thick over the rootzone. All roses benefit from good growing conditions: fertile moist soil, lots of sun, and good air circulation. Fertilize in the spring and occasionally throughout the growing season. Generally pruning can be limited to any broken or damaged branches and light tipping in the spring after growth has resumed. Maintain vigilance for typical rose pests, though they will not be troublesome on these roses.

Other Meidiland roses to consider: Ruby Meidiland—many ruby-colored flowers on compact 2 ½' to 3' plants for small gardens; White Meidiland—sparkling white 4" flowers on cascading stems.

Potential problems: black spot, mildew, and other typical rose diseases.

KNOCK OUT ROSE
Rosa Knock Out™
Category: shrub rose
Use: in mixed borders and hedges, along foundations
Soil: fertile, well-drained
Hardiness: zones 4 to 9
Mature size: 3' tall by 4' wide

Knock Out is a high-performance and low-maintenance shrub rose that works well in mixed borders, foundation plantings, or as a colorful hedge. The blue-green foliage looks good all season long and seems not to be bothered by diseases and pests, particularly black spot, which disfigures so many roses and requires a constant spray routine. The foliage turns a pleasant eggplant purple in fall, followed by orange-red rosehips, which provide winter interest. Good-sized 3" to 3 ½" single and semidouble fluorescent cherry-red flowers (with seven to eleven petals each) cover the plants from spring until frost. The plant is self-cleaning (that is, the spent flowers are shed automatically by the plant), which reduces maintenance.

This rose performs well even in very cold temperatures, down to -20 degrees Fahrenheit. It also seems not to be bothered by high humidity, a condition that adds to disease problems for many roses. It resists mildew, along with black spot, and Japanese beetles. Knock Out has received an AARS award for its high performance.

In spring, plant container specimens in fertile, well-drained soil where the plants will get five hours of sun or more for best performance. Mulch plants with about 2" of organic mulch to help prevent weed growth and keep roots cool and moist. Performance is enhanced by a constant feeding program with a slow-release fertilizer. Use liquid fertilizer when growth resumes in spring and twice more during the growing season.

For a softer color choice, a light pink version, the Blushing Knock Out rose, performs in virtually the same way.

Potential problems: black spot, mildew, and other typical rose diseases.

Knock Out rose (*Rosa* Knock Out™)

TREES

✿

SHADBLOW OR SHADBUSH
Amelanchier arborea (or *A. canadensis*)
Category: small spring flowering tree
Use: along woodland or water's edges, for naturalizing effect
Soil: moist, well-drained, fertile, acid
Hardiness: zones 3 to 8
Mature size: to 25', variable width

The shadblow is an ornamental early spring flowering native tree that can also be grown as a shrub. The common name "shadblow" is derived from the fact that the trees flower at the same time the shad run in rivers. The Latin species name is sometimes confused in the trade, but it's always a good tree. Typically this tree is found along streambanks or around ponds in the wild. It would look terrific planted similarly in cultivation, along the edge of woodlands and other naturalistic plantings or shrub borders. The flowers are white and produce a delicious fruit (if you have a few trees for pollination) that tastes a bit like blueberries; usually the birds will get it first. Bark is a decorative gray, streaked in red, and develops more character as it ages, becoming an attractive winter feature.

Transplant trees from container or balled and burlapped grown specimens into moist, acid, organic and well-drained soil where the plants will receive part shade, although they will take full sun with adequate moisture. They will adapt to poor soil conditions and seashore locations. They do not require much maintenance or pruning and can be trained as single trunk or multi-trunk plants. Some varieties to consider: 'Autumn Brilliance'—to 20' to 25', white flowers, good fall color; 'Ballerina'—to 15' to 20', white flowers, good fall color, fire blight resistant; 'Princess Diana'—to 25', white flowers, terrific fall color, single or multistemmed; 'White Pillar'—columnar to 30', fall orange-red color in fall.

Potential problems: free of most pests and deer resistant, but susceptible to fireblight, scale, and leaf spots.

HERITAGE BIRCH
Betula nigra Heritage™
Category: small, decorative tree
Use: large lawn
Soil: moist, fertile, acidic
Hardiness: zones 3 to 9
Mature size: 40' to 50' tall (20-30' common); somewhat less wide

Heritage birch is a superior trademarked variety of the common river birch, which is one of the most adaptable, dependable, and disease-free birches. The species is native to North

ABOVE: Shadbush (*Amelanchier arborea*)
BELOW: Heritage birch (*Betula nigra* Heritage™)

Redbud (*Cercis canadensis*)

America, growing along river and stream banks. This variety vastly outpaces other seedlings of the species by more than 50 percent per year and can grow 3' per year under good conditions. Young plants with trunks of only 1" to 2" in diameter start to show the wonderful white to salmon-white peeling bark that darkens and improves with age to include more brown. The clumping versions are preferred to the single trunk trees. This selection has attractive large, dark green leathery leaves.

Transplant container or balled and burlapped plants in fall or early spring, before foliage appears, into fertile, moist soil. However, Heritage birch tolerates less-than-perfect soil once established. Give it full sun for best growth, although it can take partial shade. It works well in large areas that are wet in spring or fall. Pay close attention to watering it as a young transplant and mulch with organic material (chopped leaves, compost, or bark); also water during drought. Locate it at least 20' from structures or rigid walkways as roots could become a problem. This attractive tree can be used as a specimen planting or in large scale plantings and lawns. It is very cold tolerant, having survived temperatures of -40 degrees Fahrenheit. Another river birch is Fox Valley™ ('Little King'), an 8' to 12' tall dwarf tree with decorative exfoliating bark, good for small spaces.

Potential problems: locate trees at least 20' from structures or rigid walkways to avoid roots becoming a problem.

REDBUD
Cercis canadensis
Category: small, spring flowering tree
Use: in mixed borders and woodland gardens
Soil: fertile, moist
Hardiness: zones 4 to 9 (sometimes to zone 3)
Mature size: 25' tall, typically 15'to 20', slightly wider than tall

The redbud is an adaptable small native tree, found from Canada through the southern United States, that blooms about the same time as dogwood. In fact, it can be used as a companion tree or replacement where dogwoods are challenged by disease. It flowers as a young tree, from four to six years old, with many reddish-purple buds opening rose-pink; there are color selections available. The foliage consists of attractive dark green 5" heart-shaped leaves that turn yellow in autumn.

Plant redbud in early spring or fall, from a container or balled and burlapped, into fertile, organic, well-drained soil. Redbud is less fussy once established, although it resents soggy soils. Take extra care to supply enough water until the tree is well established, as well as during times of drought, and it will produce a spring flower show second to none. A full- or part-sun location will produce the most flowers.

This native understory tree is right at home in a woodland or naturalized garden, yet works well in shrub and mixed borders and is an outstanding accent tree.

Some varieties of redbud include: 'Alba'—pure white flowers; 'Forest Pansy'—red-purple new foliage shifting to burgundy-red, then green; 'Silver Cloud'—grown for its creamy variegated leaves;

Cercis chinensis—multistemmed shrub to about 15'.

Potential problems: prune little to avoid diseases including verticillium wilt, canker, and leaf spot. Remove heavy snow to avoid damage to somewhat brittle branches.

WHITE FRINGE TREE
Chionanthus virginicus
Category: small, fragrant native tree
Use: in mixed borders
Soil: moist, fertile
Hardiness: zones 3 to 9
Mature size: variable to 25' to 30'

The white fringe tree is an adaptable and beautiful small tree, typically growing to 12' tall. It can easily be trained either as a small tree or shrub. The outstanding feature of this small tree is the elegant, drooping white flowers that are somewhat fragrant; it looks good all the time, but is incredible in flower.

This tree can spread wider than it is tall and can be used in mixed borders, massed in public plantings, or as a specimen tree. It is useful in cities as it is resistant to air pollution and could be a marvelous replacement for our troubled dogwoods. As with many American native plants, the British consider this one of the finest small trees available.

Plant white fringe tree in moist fertile soil in early spring, before new foliage appears, from small-sized container or balled and burlapped plants; some experts report problems moving or planting larger specimens. The tree grows somewhat slowly, taking from seven to ten years to reach about 10' tall.

A multistemmed cousin, the Chinese fringe tree (*Chionanthus retusus*), is also beautiful, though less hardy (zones 5 to 9). It grows a bit larger, to 15' to 25' tall, also with a spreading form. It is another excellent choice, if you have the space, and can be treated the same way.

Potential problems: relatively free from pests and disease.

DOGWOOD
Cornus 'Rutgers' hybrids
Category: spring-flowering tree
Use: in mixed borders
Soil: well-drained, fertile, sandy
Hardiness: zones 6 to 8
Mature size: 25' to 30' tall by equal width

American dogwood, *Cornus florida*, and Korean dogwood, *Cornus kousa*, are beautiful trees that are being attacked and often destroyed by diseases and pests. If you choose to plant either, pay careful attention to details, particularly planting depth (plant at depth it comes in

ABOVE: Fringe tree (*Chionanthus virginicus*)
BELOW: Rutger's hybrid dogwood (*Cornus* Stellar Pink™)

Maiden hair tree (*Ginkgo biloba*)

container, not lower), moisture (well-drained soil), and light (full sun or small amount of shade). Overwatering or soggy soil will certainly kill all dogwoods, yet they need water to become established and in time of drought. Feed young trees one-third strength of a balanced slow-release fertilizer. Mulch trees with 2" to 3" of organic matter to the dripline of the tree but not up against the trunk. Following those rules will give you a better chance of success.

You can improve the odds even more by planting one of the new Rutgers hybrid dogwoods developed by Dr. Elwin Orton. Each of these trees is more pest and disease resistant and more vigorous than the parent species. These multiseason varieties flower about one week later than *C. florida*, and one or two weeks earlier than *C. kousa*. They have typical outstanding red fall foliage; because of their sterility, they do not produce fruit. They also tend to be deer resistant. These hybrids will reach about 25' to 30' tall at maturity, and about 15' tall in 15 years, depending on growing conditions.

Hybrids include: Aurora™—upright habit with white, tight bracts; Celestial™—full tree, white with overlapping bracts; Constellation™—upright habit with white, open bracts; Ruth Ellen™—spreading habit, more like *C. florida*, with large white bracts; Stellar Pink—vigorous upright habit with rounded pink and white overlapping bracts.

Potential problems: deer, pest, and disease resistant.

MAIDENHAIR
Ginkgo biloba
Category: decorative tree
Use: along streets
Soil: well-drained, fertile
Hardiness: zones 3 to 8
Mature size: 40' to 80', width varies

The maidenhair tree is one of the most ancient trees. The beautiful medium-green fan-shaped leaves, which resemble a maidenhair fern, turn yellow-gold most autumns and then drop from the tree simultaneously on the first freeze. The elegant leaf form is often used as inspiration in art and jewelry making. The ginkgo is tolerant of a wide range of conditions, so it is quite adaptable to city street plantings. It is a wonderful specimen tree any place there is room. Select only male clones (buy only labeled, named plants) so you will not have the malodorous fruit produced by the female, though it is highly prized in Asian communities. Trees take more than 20 years, perhaps as long as 50 years, to reach flowering and fruiting stage and become more elegant with age.

Plant container-grown specimens in spring into deep, well-drained, fertile, sandy soil in full sun. However, they tolerate less-than-perfect conditions once established. Young trees are rather pyramidal in shape but broaden as they get older. Prune as necessary when young. Seed-grown plants sold as the species will be variable in shape and size; cultivated varieties are more consistent in both.

Varieties of maidenhair include: 'Autumn Gold'—rounded cone shape, 50' tall by 30' wide, no fruit; 'Magyar'—narrow pyramid shape with strong central leader, good branching, great fall color, no fruit; 'Mariken'—globe shaped, tight branching structure, grafted, and does not produce fruit; 'Princeton Sentry'—upright, somewhat columnar, slightly tapered symmetrical branching, no fruit.

Potential problems: virtually no problems if you have the space.

GROUND COVERS

PLUMBAGO
Ceratostigma plumbaginoides
Category: flowering lawn alternative
Use: for edges, front of borders (without foot traffic)
Soil: well-drained, fertile
Hardiness: zones 5 to 10
Mature size: 8" to 12" tall by 12" to 18"

Plumbago is a durable, spreading, deciduous ground cover dense enough to prevent most weeds from growing through. Bright green foliage emerges late in spring, followed by highly desirable, deep gentian blue flowers at the end of summer that persist into fall. As flower petals drop off, red calyxes start to show and offer contrast. Foliage turns a decorative and brilliant red bronze with colder temperatures and persists into late fall. You can also use it in the front of a mixed border or as an edge plant in a rock garden. Plant the area with very early bulbs, such as daffodils, that will grow and bloom before plumbago growth resumes. The fresh growth will cover the fading bulb foliage.

In the northern end of its growing range, plant plumbago in full sun in average, well-drained fertile soil. Start with container or bare-root plants, spacing about 18" apart. Water well until the plants are established. In cold areas, cut plants to the ground after first frost; other places, cut to the ground in early spring to encourage new growth. In zones 5 and 6, protect plants by applying a couple inches of loose, organic mulch after the first frost.

Potential problems: few disease and pest problems; winter wet can cause root rot.

Plumbago (*Ceratostigma plumbaginoides*)

ABOVE: Barrenwort (*Epimedium* x *perralchicum* 'Frohnleiten')
BELOW: Russian cypress (*Microbiota decussata*)

BARRENWORT, BISHOP'S HAT
Epimedium x *perralchicum* 'Frohnleiten'
Category: dry shade ground cover
Use: grass alternative (without foot traffic)
Soil: moist to dry
Hardiness: zones 5 to 9
Mature size: 1' high by 1' wide

Frohnleiten' is a sturdy, quickly established, low-maintenance ground cover for shaded areas. Bright yellow flowers are produced in May to June or appear soon after cutting back, followed by fresh green foliage with a bronze-red edge. This ground cover remains reliably evergreen in zones 6 to 9 and looks great most of the year.

'Frohnleiten' performs well in moist, organic soils and even in challenging dry-shade locations. Optimal growing conditions will improve growth, and plants will reach a height of about 12" and will spread to 12" wide. For fast coverage, plant 3" pot-sized plants 6" to 8" apart. Plants spaced 12" apart will fill in more slowly. Water plants regularly until well established. Cut plants down to the ground in the spring; use a weed whacker or lawn mower in large areas.

Another ground cover for shade is Japanese spurge (*Pachysandra terminalis* 'Green Sheen'), a very shiny-leaved evergreen that looks attractive all year long. Its foliage is about 6" to 8" tall and is tolerant of sun, with enough moisture, but best in partial shade. Space new plantings 8" apart and keep well watered.

Potential problems: deer resistant with few pest problems.

RUSSIAN CYPRESS, RUSSIAN ARBORVITAE
Microbiota decussata
Category: evergreen grass alternative
Use: lawns (without foot traffic)
Soil: average to lean, well-drained
Hardiness: zones 3 to 8
Mature size: 12" tall by several feet wide, ultimately to 12'

Russian cypress makes an interesting replacement for junipers. Because of its Siberian heritage, Russian cypress can take a lot of cold, probably to -40 degrees Fahrenheit. The pleasing green color changes to bronzy-purple in the fall. The plants will attain a height of about 12" to 16" and will grow horizontally (8" to 12" annually) to reach a spread of 12' over many years. For a more filled-in look, space container-grown plants about 3' to 5' apart, then remove plants as they spread and grow into each other. Russian cyprus also works in a raised planter where it can spill over the sides.

In the spring, plant container-grown specimens in well-drained soils in full sun. Plants can withstand dry conditions or a bit of shade. However, they do best in full sun with adequate moisture when in active growth. In dryer locations, water well until plants are established; afterward plants will take far less water and can withstand drought. You can prune in early spring but only remove small quantities of growth during any season as it does not tolerate heavy pruning. It has won awards from two programs, the Long Island Gold Medal and Cary plant award programs.

Potential problems: no known pests and diseases, but winter wet locations will destroy the plants.

VINES

✣

CLIMBING HYDRANGEA
Hydrangea anomala subsp. *Petiolaris*
Category: flowering climber
Use: for arbors, rock walls, climbing over hardscape
Soil: well-drained, moist
Hardiness: zones 4 to 8
Mature size: 60' to 70' tall

Climbing hydrangea is an attractive clinging plant that can reach 60' to 70' in height at maturity. It can also be trained to much lower levels to cover a rock pile, sturdy arbor, or brick, rock, or masonry wall. You also can train it as an unusual ground cover or allow it to climb into a tree. This vine has four-season interest, with large flat, lacy, and fragrant white flowers lasting more than four weeks beginning in late June into July. The dark green glossy foliage looks great over the entire growing season, becomes golden in the fall, and then loses its leaves to expose its red-brown exfoliating bark, which provides both structure and interest throughout winter.

Climbing hydrangea is slow to start and takes several years to really grow well, but after that it is quite vigorous and well worth the time needed to establish itself. Plant this climber in spring from a container and supply adequate moisture until it takes off. Loosely tie the vine where you want it to grow. This is necessary only until the vine grows and its root-like structures hold on. You must plan for the future since this vine gets very heavy with age and could damage wooden structures or mortar. In cold areas, it will perform best on eastern- and northern-facing walls. It thrives in full sun, yet is adaptable to partial shade locations and works well in seashore locations. It is a Long Island Gold Medal and Cary Award winner.

Potential problems: few serious disease and insect problems.

Climbing hydrangea (*Hydrangea anomala* subsp. *Petiolaris*)

ABOVE: Sweet potato vine 'Marguerite' (*Ipomoea batatas* 'Marguerite' ['Margarita'])
BELOW: Blue fescue (*Festuca ovina* var. *glauca*)

SWEET POTATO VINE
Ipomoea batatas 'Blackie'
Category: annual climber
Use: in containers and window boxes
Soil: moist, well-drained, fertile
Hardiness: annual in New England
Mature size: 6" to 12" tall; can trail 10'

Sweet potato 'Blackie' has become popular in recent years because it is easy to grow and is distinctive with its purple-black, deeply cut, "bird's footprint" leaves. It can be used in containers, window boxes, or as a ground cover. Combine with other color forms of sweet potato, silver- or yellow-leaved or flowered plants such as dichondra, lamb's ears, strawflower, and wormwood for striking contrasts. The tubers are edible but better used to grow decorative plants.

Transplant container-grown plants or start tubers in fertile, well-drained soil in sun or part-sun locations and give adequate moisture. Cuttings can be rooted for additional plants. "Pinching" the vines—cutting individual vines back at points just beyond a pair of leaves—will make the plants more robust and less stringy. Plants grow rapidly in warm weather.

Feed the vines monthly with balanced liquid fertilizer or incorporate time-release fertilizer in the planting mix in containers. For ground cover use, plants can be spaced 2' apart in well-prepared, fertile soil. Pinch back after rapid growth has begun and feed monthly. Sweet potato vines may be treated as annuals or wintered over indoors as potted plants.

Other sweet potato varieties include: 'Ace of Spades'—large, heart-shaped, purple-black leaves, heat loving, slower growing than 'Blackie'; 'Marguerite'—large chartreuse or lime-green leaves; 'Tricolor'—large pink, green, and white variegated leaves.

Potential problems: spider mites are sometimes a problem for plants in hot locations that are not well watered.

GRASSES

BLUE FESCUE
Festuca ovina glauca
Category: perennial grass
Use: for edges, mixed borders, and rock gardens
Soil: very well-drained, average or lean
Hardiness: zones 4 to 9
Mature size: 10" by 10"

This popular grass has silvery-blue leaves that arch gracefully into about a 10" mound that remains evergreen in the warm end of its growing range. It can be used as a ground cover, although it will require some weeding between plants. It also works well at the edge of other plantings or in a rock garden. Blue fescue combines well with virtually any color, although looks best with cool shades of blue, pastels, or in contrast to dark foliage. Its fine leaves also contrast with the texture of most annuals and perennials. It looks good in container plantings, but does not winter over well.

For best results, grow blue fescue in full sun in rather lean, even poor, well-drained soil. It will take a bit of shade, but in all cases avoid overwatering and heavy summer mulching with organic mulches. For rock gardens, mulch with gravel. About every three years divide plants, which will help maintain good color and avoid dead areas in their centers. If plants heave or push out of the ground, dig them up, divide them, and reset them. *Festuca cinerea, F. glauca,* and *F. arvensis* are all synonyms for *Festuca ovina glauca.*

Cultivars of fescues: 'Elijah's Blue'—icy blue leaves, 10″ mound; 'Silver Lining'—silver-blue leaves, 10″ tall; 'Soiling'—blue-gray leaves in spring and summer, then red-brown, 8″ tall; 'Tom Thumb'—silver-blue leaves in spring, green in summer, 4″ tall; *Festuca amethystina*—blue-green mounds, 12″ tall, fine-textured leaves.

Potential problems: virtually the only problem with blue fescue is crown rot, which results from too much mulch and water.

BLUE SWITCH GRASS
Panicum virgatum 'Heavy Metal'
Category: perennial grass
Use: in mixed borders, winter gardens, along seashore
Soil: average, well-drained
Hardiness: zones 5 to 9
Mature size: 4' to 5' tall by about half as wide

Blue switch grass makes an excellent addition to mixed and naturalistic borders or bird gardens. The dramatic 4' to 5' tall waxy blue-green blades create vertical interest in most borders and work well with perennials in a naturalistic garden and by the seashore. Although it is a clumping grass, it is light and airy in the garden. Fall produces a color shift to bright yellow; the attractive burgundy seedheads weigh down the blades and bend them into a graceful weeping look in winter. The chickadees love these for the seed. Blue switch grass offers visual interest in virtually every month of the year.

Plant container-grown or bare-root specimens in spring into average, well-drained soil in full sun about 3' apart. This grass is tolerant of sandy to wet conditions and performs well in hot summer conditions. 'Heavy Metal' looks spectacular when backlit late in the year. If grown in more shade, plants are much more likely to flop over and require staking. Cut back nearly to the ground in late winter to prepare the plants for spring's new growth.

Potential problems: usually pest free.

Blue switch grass (*Panicum virgatum* 'Heavy Metal')

BLUE LYME GRASS, BLUE WILD RYE
Elymus arenarius 'Glaucus'
Category: perennial grass
Use: in mixed borders, for erosion control, along seashore
Soil: dry to wet
Hardiness: zones 3 to 10
Mature size: 1' to 2' tall by 2' to 3' wide

Blue lyme grass is an effective, attractive, and vigorous blue-gray perennial that produces a lovely contrast for most plants in a mixed border and is outstanding enough to be a specimen planting. It may be the most intense blue of any plant available. Because it is tolerant of a wide range of conditions, thrives in heat, and spreads via rhizomes, it is a good choice for erosion control and dune plantings in seashore locations. This adaptability can be a liability in places with good soil and growing conditions; there it can get out of control, so gardeners must keep an eye on it. It is easiest to control in difficult and challenging growing conditions: very wet or very dry soils.

Plant container-grown or bare-root plants about 4' apart in spring in full sun or partial shade. Blue lyme grass can also be planted in a large, bottomless planter or giant nursery pot with the bottom removed, placed with the top rim at ground level or slightly above; this will help keep the rhizomes from spreading outward.

Combine and contrast with any or all of the following: *Sedum* x *telephium* 'Autumn Joy'—succulent; green to rosy-red "broccoli-flowers" in fall, to 2' tall; *Pennisetum alopecuroides* 'Moudry'—black foxtail-like flower spikes; *Penstemon digitalis* 'Husker Red'—dark, red-black leaves, to 3' tall.

Potential problems: virtually no disease or pest problems.

HERBS AND EDIBLES

CHIVES
Allium schoenoprasum
Category: perennial herb
Use: in vegetable or colonial gardens
Soil: moist, well-drained, and moderately fertile
Hardiness: zones 3 to 9
Mature size: 18" tall by 18" wide

Early colonists transported chives with them to the United States and grew them in their gardens. Bunches of chives were hung on doors to ward off evil spirits. With its jaunty globes of lavender flowers, this showy herb can be the star of any herb garden and hold its own in early

ABOVE: Blue lyme grass (*Elymus arenarius* 'Glaucus')
BELOW: Chives (*Allium schoenoprasum*)

Lettuce (*Lactuca sativa*)

spring with other perennials or annuals. Chives are suitable for period or historic gardens along with more traditional herb and vegetable gardens, mixed borders, and can be used in containers.

Both the organically grown leaves and flowers of chives are edible and have a mild onion flavor, working well with eggs, potatoes, and most vegetables. Snip the bright green narrow spiky leaves any time they are over 6" tall. Chives freeze well: cut leaves, freeze separated on sheet, then seal tightly in container; use as you would fresh-cut leaves. Prior to use, separate flower globes into individual florets to sprinkle on salads and vegetables.

Start from seed in containers, purchase plants, or ask a friend who grows them to give you a starter; the latter will always have some to share. Grow in full sun in moist, well-drained, moderately fertile soil. Plants will spread if flowers are allowed to go to seed, so cut back after flowering. Plants benefit from dividing every three years or so. They contrast well with purple plants like purple basil. Cut clumps to about 1" above ground, leaving some areas standing so chive leaves are always available for cooking and use.

Other chives include: 'Forsgate'—pink flowered form of garden chives; *A. tuberosum*—garlic chives, a tasty but voracious spreader.

Potential problems: rarely troubled by any pests or diseases.

LETTUCE
Lactuca sativa
Category: annual vegetable
Use: in containers and vegetable gardens, for decorative edging
Soil: average
Hardiness: annual in New England
Mature size: to about 10" tall

Lettuce is a simple, rewarding vegetable to grow in spring or fall, any time the ground is cool, ideally around 60 degrees Fahrenheit. There are four basic types of lettuce: leaf, butterhead or Boston, romaine, and iceberg. The latter is not well-suited to the home garden, with little to offer beyond crunch anyway. Leaf lettuce is the best and easiest lettuce for home gardeners. It grows into a very loose head in rather poor soil in warmer weather. All lettuce is best grown in temperatures between 60 degrees and 75 degrees Fahrenheit with adequate water and potassium in the soil. Romaine, or cos lettuce, grows into stiff, upright, crunchy, and juicy leaves with significant flavor. Butterhead forms a soft head of tasty lettuce that is not conducive to shipping, so is usually only available to home growers. Mesclun is a mix of varied edible leaves harvested when small and tender, and is treated the same as lettuce.

As soon as soil can be worked in spring, sow seed about 1" apart in rows spread 18" apart. As plants grow, snip for salads and thin out plants until leaf lettuce is 6" apart and butterhead 10". You can broadcast-sow, sprinkling seed evenly across a few feet of soil. In all cases, cover seed with about 1/8" of soil and keep well watered; grow in full sun or partial shade. For continuous harvesting, you should plant seed every three to four weeks through entire growing season; plant heat-resistant varieties in summer.

Varieties of lettuce include: butterhead (harvest in 65 to 75 days)—'Buttercrunch', 'Summer

English lavender (*Lavandula angustifolia* 'Hidcote')

Bibb'; leaf lettuce (harvest in 45 to 50 days)—'Red Sails', 'Oakleaf', and 'Red Salad Bowl'; Romaine (harvest in 75 to 85 days)—'Parris Island Cos', 'Little Caesar', and 'Freckles'.

Potential problems: may include aphids and cabbage looper.

ENGLISH LAVENDER
Lavandula angustifolia 'Hidcote'
Category: fragrant perennial herb
Use: in containers and vegetable gardens
Soil: very well-drained, sandy loam
Hardiness: zones 5 to 8
Mature size: about 16" to 24" tall; a bit less wide

Lavender is a very fragrant woody herb that should be grown in full sun in very well-drained soil, as in its Mediterranean home of origin. The silvery leaves are aromatic and are often used for scenting linen and in potpourris. The scent is unusual as it can be both stimulating and relaxing—a favorite with aromatherapists, a simple pleasure for the rest of us. Lavender is useful in an herb or vegetable garden. 'Hidcote' is a compact grower with deep purple-blue flowers. It is suitable for any low-water or xeriscape garden and works well with roses or in contrast to dark foliage plants.

Transplant lavender from containers in spring, watering well until the plants are firmly established; then avoid overwatering. Mulch plants after the ground freezes. Well-established plants need water infrequently; but water deeply. Fertilize in spring with a balanced fertilizer. Cut stems just before flowers are totally open or cut back hard, removing one-third to one-half of the plant after flowering has finished. In the second year of growth, it is fine to cut flowers and cut back plants after flowering. To dry stems: cut, bundle with rubber bands, and hang upside down in a cool, dry, and dark location.

Other lavenders include: 'Lavender Lady'—often behaves as an annual, flowering the first year; *Lavandula stoechas*—Spanish lavender with large purple flowers (bracts); *Lavandula dentata*—French lavender with narrow, gray-green leaves with decorative serrated edge; *Lavandula* x *intermedia*—fragrant varieties include 'Provence' and 'Grosso'; 'Munstead Dwarf'—to 12" tall, violet-blue flowers.

Potential problems: winter wet conditions are fatal to lavender.

ABOVE: Tomato 'Celebrity' (*Lycopersicon esculentum* 'Celebrity')
BELOW: Basil (*Ocimum basilicum*)

TOMATO
Lycopersicon esculentum
Category: annual vegetable
Use: small varieties in containers
Soil: evenly moist, fertile, organic
Hardiness: annual in New England
Mature size: varies

The tomato is a favorite vegetable that is easy to grow in virtually unlimited varieties. Choose cherry, grape, pear, and plum shapes in orange, black, green, striped, pink, and red. Select them in sizes from tiny types no bigger than your fingertip to giant multi-pound varieties.

Grow all tomatoes in good, moist, fertile, organic soil in full sun. Keep evenly moist throughout the growing season. Use organic mulch at the base of plants to keep plants clean, moist, and help avoid disease; avoid high-nitrogen fertilizers. Start seed indoors four to six weeks before the last frost date for your region; then plant out seedlings two weeks later, or purchase plants. Use stakes, a trellis, or a cage for tall-growing indeterminate varieties; this is optional with determinate tomatoes. Leave 2' to 3' between supported plants, more if allowed to sprawl.

Some varieties and their uses, including days to maturity after planting out, are: **Small fruit/cherry:** 'Super Sweet 100'—65 days, indeterminate, stake them, extra sweet; 'Tiny Tim'— 50 days, determinate, small ½" fruit, 15" tall plants, use in containers. **Slicing:** 'Better Boy'—75 days, indeterminate, red, firm, flavorful; 'Brandywine'—78 days, indeterminate, pink, large; 'Early Girl'—52 days, indeterminate, red; **Tomato paste:** 'Banana Legs'—75 days, determinate, bright yellow and 4" long banana shape; 'Roma'—76 days, determinate; **Other colors:** 'Black Krim'— 69 days, indeterminate, almost black fruit, sweet; 'Lemon Boy'—72 days, indeterminate, yellow fruit; 'Yellow Pear'—78 days, indeterminate, yellow pear 1-ounce fruit.

Potential problems: Keep moist to prevent blossom-end rot, pick off hornworms, and select disease-resistant varieties to prevent and control most problems. Letters after the name indicate specific disease resistance; VFT indicates resistance to verticillium wilt, fusarium wilt, and tobacco mosaic virus.

BASIL
Ocimum basilicum
Category: annual herb
Use: for edging, in containers, cooking
Soil: moist
Hardiness: annual in New England
Mature size: varies from 8" tall to over 24" tall

Basil is an easily grown, decorative, tasty, and historic plant known from the 1600s forward. In early times, it was primarily used for medicinal purposes, although today's gardeners and cooks value it for the pungent accent it adds to fresh-cut tomatoes, in sauces, or to freshly prepared pesto. Use basil in the herb garden, vegetable garden, and in containers. Dwarf basil

Snowdrops (*Galanthus nivalis*)

works as an edger; purple basil complements silver or green foliage. Grow a few plants in pots in a sunny windowsill in winter.

Grow basil in good garden soil in full sun. Start seed indoors about five weeks before the average frost date in spring or sow directly in garden when soil temperatures reach 60 degrees Fahrenheit; basil does not like cool temperatures. Some varieties are available as nursery plants in early spring.

The four basic types of basil are the sweet green basil, dwarf green basil, purple-leaved basil, and scented-leaf basil. Sweet basil grows to about 2' tall and has 2" to 3" long leaves; it has closely related cousins, including the even larger lettuce-leaf basil, whose leaves are sometimes used for wrapping other foods. Dwarf basil grows to about 12" tall and has smaller ½" leaves. 'Spicy Globe' and 'Green Bouquet' grow naturally into rounded globe shapes. Purple-leaved basil is very decorative with ruffled, frilled, or deeply cut leaves with very pungent flavors. Popular varieties include two All-America Selection winners, 'Purple Ruffles' and 'Red Rubin'. Scented-leaf basil adds another aroma to the typical clove-anise basil scent. 'Sweet Dani', an AAS winner, is distinctly lemon flavored and has gray-green leaves. Cinnamon basil has a spicy cinnamon scent and flavor, and anise basil smells like licorice.

Potential problems: few pests or problems.

BULBS

SNOWDROPS
Galanthus nivalis
Category: perennial bulb
Use: for deciduous woodland gardens, lawns
Soil: well-drained
Hardiness: zones 3 to 8
Mature size: 4" to 8" tall, spreading

Snowdrops are the most welcome harbinger of spring in New England, blooming far earlier than virtually any other plant. They are not fazed by a small snowfall and make us smile by poking their cheery little white ½" flowers above the winter blanket. They are equally welcomed without the snow and look great in lawns and under deciduous shrubs and trees.

Snowdrops are best planted in significant numbers; twenty-something minimum, though several hundred will make an impact. You should plant the bulbs about 4" deep and 2" to 3" apart; or about eight bulbs per square foot. To produce a naturalized look, dig a bed 4" deep in the area you wish to plant, or in lawns "peel" back the sod to that depth, then scatter the bulbs. Plant most of them just where they land. This is the best way to plant hundreds of these small gems. They can be moved in spring as flowers start to fade. Some years, fertilize with bulb fertilizer in the fall and when growth resumes in the spring. Well-drained soil is a must. Allow foliage to turn yellow before cutting it off; for large numbers of bulbs, cut off with a lawn mower. They require little care and get better year after year in the garden.

Other snowdrops to consider: 'Flore Pleno'—double flowered snowdrop; *G. elwesii*—giant snowdrop, earlier blooming, 12" tall with 1 ½" flowers.

Potential problems: virtually pest and disease free, but winter wet soil will kill these bulbs.

LILIES
Lilium spp.
Category: perennial bulb
Use: in borders, cut flowers
Soil: fertile, moist, well-drained
Hardiness: zones 4 to 8
Mature size: varies from 2' to 6' tall

Lilies are the aristocrats of the bulb world, with a wide range of large, colorful, and wonderfully scented flowers. Distinct groups include Aurelian, Asiatic, and Oriental hybrids. The Asiatic lilies are the earliest hybrids to bloom and have brightly colored flowers generally 4" to 6" wide, with flat or open faces; most, though not all, face upward and often have dark spots in the throat. Colors include pink, red, orange, yellow, and white. They do well in zones 4 to 7. The Aurelian hybrids bloom after the Asiatic hybrids, with large fragrant flowers about 6" to 8" long and up to 8" wide. Flowers can be peach, pink, orange, yellow, and greenish-white; often they have yellow throats or maroon stripes. Plants grow about 4' to 6' tall. The Oriental hybrids are the last to bloom and their rich scent and lush appearance reward the gardener for the wait. They have large flowers 6" to 12" wide in shades of pink, red, and white on plants that grow from 2' to 7' tall.

Plant lily bulbs in the fall before frost in groups of three, five, or more in fertile, moist, and well-drained soil. It is best to have the tops of the plants in sun, but the "feet" or bulbs in the shade of other plants. You should mulch growing plants with 1" or more of organic matter in spring. Plants perform best when you allow the flowers to open in the garden and remain on the plants, removing only the old flower when it is past its prime. If you cut flowers with many leaves, plants often do not bloom the next season and may even die. When leaves die at the end of season, cut stems an inch or so above the ground. This reminds you where they are in the garden. Remove pollen sacks from flowers to avoid staining clothing and skin.

Potential problems: rodents, slugs, and snails.

Lily 'Casa Blanca' (*Lilium* 'Casa Blanca')

DAFFODIL
Narcissus 'Dutch Master'
Category: perennial bulb
Use: in woodland or naturalized gardens
Soil: well-drained
Hardiness: zones 3 to 9
Mature size: 15" to 18"

Daffodils are among the easiest and most rewarding of all perennial plants; the large-flowered forms produce lots of color year after year with a minimum of work. 'Dutch Master' is an old favorite occasionally mislabeled 'King Alfred', which produces small yellow daffodils instead of the large and magnificent bright yellow flowers.

Plant daffodils in the fall in well-drained soil in sunny locations or in deciduous woodland areas under trees and shrubs that lose their leaves in winter. Plant bulbs to a depth about three times the height of each bulb, pointy side up, flat side down. Planted in the right location, daffodils will bloom for years and years with almost no care. Use bulb fertilizer in the fall and in spring when they resume growth. When they have finished blooming and the foliage has turned yellow, simply cut it off. Daffodils are best planted in sweeps or drifts along hillsides or borders; plant as many as you can. You create a stronger visual statement by planting many, 50 to 100, or even 500 of a single variety in a border or single location. The older hybrids like 'Dutch Master' are very affordable in large quantities. Daffodils can also be interplanted with daylilies and lilies in sun, or with hellebores and ferns in shade. The daffodils bloom early in the season; the other plants then grow and cover the ripening foliage.

Other daffodils to consider: 'Tete-a-Tete'—10" miniature yellow flowers early in spring; 'Thalia'—15" tall milky-white fragrant flowers, three to a stem.

Potential problems: virtually no enemies; even deer and squirrels rarely eat or disturb them.

ANNUALS

BACHELOR'S BUTTON, CORNFLOWER
Centaurea cyanus
Category: flowering annual
Use: massed in borders, cottage gardens, meadows, and edges
Soil: well-drained, sandy loam
Hardiness: annual in New England
Mature size: 1' to 3' tall

Bachelor's button and cornflowers are among the most popular flowers. They are called cornflowers because they grow wild in the cornfields of Europe. They are a favorite of children,

ABOVE: Daffodil 'Dutch Master' (*Narcissus* 'Dutch Master')
BELOW: Bachelor's button mix (*Centaurea cyanus*)

Cosmos 'Sensation' mix (*Cosmos bipinnatus* 'Sensation' series)

who often find they are so easy to grow. Their perky, yet delicate, 1 ½ to 2" flowers brighten summer gardens. They work well massed or woven throughout other plants or can be used in cottage gardens and meadows. Their distinctive gray-green foliage makes them an attractive edging plant. Varieties include blue, pink, white, and purple flowers in heights of 1' to 3' tall. Cornflowers often self-sow to provide plants for future years. Tall varieties can be supported by more rigid companion plants such as poppies.

Grow cornflowers in full sun or light shade in well-drained sandy loam. Fertilize growing plants once in the spring. In the garden, sow seed in the fall for plants that will flower the following spring. Indoors, sow seed in containers four to six weeks before the last frost date in the spring, or directly into prepared soil in the garden as soon as the soil can be worked.

The other popular cornflower is *C. cineraria*, the famed silver-leaved plant used for contrast with dark foliage plants in borders or containers. It grows 6" to 18" tall and equally wide and, although it is a perennial, it is also best treated as an annual.

Some varieties of cornflowers include: 'Blue Boy'—2' to 3' tall, blue flowers; 'Blue Midget'— 10" mounds of sky blue flowers; 'Jubilee Gem'—1' tall, deep blue flowers; 'Polka Dot'—15" tall, blue, crimson, and white flowers.

Potential problems: aphids are sometimes a problem.

COSMOS
Cosmos bipinnatus
Category: flowering annual
Use: massed in borders
Soil: well-drained, lean or average
Hardiness: annual in New England
Mature size: 3' to 6' tall by 2' wide

Cosmos adds a light, almost airy touch to gardens whether massed at the back of borders or woven through other plants. The soft, ferny, fine-textured foliage works well with virtually any other flower, whether in the border or a vase. Cosmos is a fine, long-lasting cut flower. The saucer-shaped flowers resemble delicate, open daisies and come in pastel shades of pink, rose, magenta, crimson, and white. The taller varieties may need staking, particularly in windy sites; or plant them where nearby sturdy plants will support them.

Easy and very fast to grow from seed, cosmos can be directly sown in prepared, well-drained lean soil. Very rich and fertile soil will promote more leaf growth than flower growth. You also can sow seed in containers four weeks before your planting out date. Cosmos are easy to transplant; set seedlings about 1' apart. Cosmos frequently self-sows in the garden for lots of "volunteers" for future years. Yellow cosmos (*Cosmos sulphureus*) does not transplant well and should be left to grow where it is originally sown. Full sun is best to keep the plants from stretching and getting too lanky; pinching back early in their growth will also help. Be careful not to overwater and do not fertilize cosmos.

Varieties of cosmos: 'Bright Lights'—3' tall, very intense colors; 'Early Wonder' series—mixed colors, 3' tall, large flowers; 'Red Versailles'—striking red, 4' tall; 'Seashells'—pink, white, or two-toned tubular flower petals, 3½' tall; 'Sensation' series—mixed colors, 3' to 6' tall; 'Sonata' series—mixed colors, 2' tall, bushy.

Potential problems: generally problem-free, although occasionally bothered by aphids or Japanese beetles.

CORN POPPY, SHIRLEY POPPY
Papaver rhoeas
Category: flowering annual
Use: massed or as color accent
Soil: well-drained, average to poor
Hardiness: annual in New England
Mature size: 1' to 3' tall

The corn poppies are famous for their attractive, ferny foliage and bright, paper-thin petals marked with spots of white. These are also the famous poppies of Flanders Field. The flower colors range from red, purple, and pink to pastel shades of blue and apricot, with some varieties having doubled petals. Reverend W. Wilks of Shirley, England, started selecting specific color types, all having a white base and ranging from white through red, orange, and pink shades, some double; these are called Shirley poppies.

The flowers seem delicate as they wave in soft breezes in the summer garden and make beautiful cut flowers; singe the cut end of the stem with a match or lighter to extend the life of the bouquet. These graceful plants work well massed for dramatic effect or sprinkled throughout a meadow or mixed border. They often will self-sow where grown, thus providing serendipitous color in future years; these plants are often unusually vigorous.

In cold climates, sow seed as soon as soil can be worked in spring; then sow additional seed a few weeks later for a longer bloom season. In warmer areas, sow seed in fall for flowers the next year. Poppies resent transplanting, so sow them where they will grow or start in peat pots so roots will not be disturbed when they are planted into the garden. Grow them in full sun in soil that is a bit lean and do not fertilize. Poppy seeds are tiny and can be mixed with fine dry sand to make sowing more controlled. Thin out the weakest growing seedlings to about 9" apart. Most other poppies can be grown the same way.

Potential problems: aphids, whiteflies, and powdery mildew can occasionally be a problem.

Corn poppy (*Papaver rhoeas*)

ABOVE: Petunia hybrids (*Petunia* x *hybrida*)
BELOW: Salvia 'Blue Bedder' (*Salvia farinacea* 'Blue Bedder')

PETUNIA
Petunia x hybrida
Category: flowering annual
Use: in borders, containers, edges
Soil: average to fertile, well-drained
Hardiness: annual in New England
Mature size: to 24" tall

Petunias are popular plants for adding color to our landscapes and gardens from late spring until frost. Virtually every color is available: red, pink, magenta, lavender, purple, and salmon, with variations such as ruffles and fancy edges, stripes, or dark, decorative veins. Flower size varies from under 1" to more than 5" across. Use them in borders, as ground covers, in hanging baskets, window boxes, and other containers for decks, and for spot color anywhere. They can provide bright accents to the edges of borders.

Plant petunias outside after danger of frost is past in decent, moist, well-drained soil in full sun or with some shade. Although tolerant of less-than-ideal conditions, petunias produce best results with better organic soils and full sun. Water and fertilize regularly, deadhead (remove spent flowers), and keep tidy by shaping and pruning as needed.

Types of petunias: **Grandifloras**—largest flowers to 4 1 ½' across, some ruffled or fringed, plants to 27" high, spread of 3', best in containers; strains include 'Fluffy Ruffles', 'Supermagic', 'Hula-hoop', 'Frost', and 'Cascade'. **Millifloras**—more compact plants with many smaller flowers, about 2" wide, singles or doubles; strains include the 'Fantasy' series, which come in blue, pink, red, and white. **Multifloras**—more but smaller, denser flowers, singles and doubles, good in garden and containers; strains include 'Celebrity', 'Primetime', and 'Merlin'. **Trailing**—these spreading plants are good for containers; the 'Wave' series can spread 5' but only 6" tall, 'Surfinias' are similar with 1 ½" flowers, 'Petitunias' are the smallest at ¾", and 'Supertunias' are the largest with up to 2½"-wide flowers.

Potential problems: a root disease called pythium and whiteflies can sometimes be problems.

MEALYCUP SAGE
Salvia farinacea
Category: flowering annual
Use: massed or in containers
Soil: well-drained, average
Hardiness: annual in New England
Mature size: 15" to 24" tall by 10" wide

The mealycup sage blooms all summer long and into fall on airy and upright stems. The species includes lavender flowers, along with white, blue, and bicolor selections and hybrids. The common name, mealycup, comes from the leaf-like cup or calyx that holds flowers and appears as if it was dusted in flour. This sage, with its attractive gray-green foliage, looks good massed in a border or in containers.

Marigold (*Tagetes erecta* 'First Lady')

This Texas native grows well in full sun in average, well-drained soil. Water during droughts and feed sparingly. It is often available at the nursery early in spring, or you can grow it from seed sown about ten weeks before the last frost date and left uncovered in a 75 degree Fahrenheit location. Space seedling plants about 12" apart in the garden. You should deadhead, removing spent flowers, to prolong bloom. Mealycup sage is generally an easy plant with few problems; though you may have occasional problems with damping off of seedlings.

Mealycup sage varieties include: 'Blue Bedder'—16" tall, deep blue flowers; 'Silver White'—18" tall, white flowers; 'Strata'—14" to 18" tall, blue and white bicolor, All American Selection award winner. 'Victoria'—18" tall, violet blue flowers; 'White Bedder'—14" tall, white flowers;

Other sages: *S. coccinea* 'Lady in Red'—All American Selection; *S. officinalis*—perennial herb used for the seasoning; *S. splendens*—common red annual, although also comes in pink, white, and purple.

Potential problems: aphids in mature plants; less prone to slug damage than *S. splendens.*

MARIGOLD
Tagetes spp.
Category: flowering annual
Use: in borders, containers, vegetable and herb gardens
Soil: moist, well-drained
Hardiness: annual in New England
Mature plant size: 1' to 3', about the same width

Marigolds are popular because they are bright, cheery, easy to grow, and have few problems. Virtually every color choice is available in various heights; mass them in borders, as edgers, for containers, and include some types in vegetable and herb gardens. They can be used almost anywhere in the garden and most are suitable for cutting, although some people find their scent unpleasant.

Most marigolds do well in moist, well-drained soil in full sun. However, many will do well in less-than-perfect spots. They are easy to grow from seed, although some types are available as nursery plants in spring. Sow seed in containers about six to eight weeks before your last frost date. Small varieties can be sown outdoors where they are to grow in late spring; all are easy to transplant. Marigolds are terrific plants for children; the kids will get much enjoyment from planting and tending them and learn about nature and gardening through the process. Water plants in time of drought, fertilize lightly, and deadhead (remove old flowers) throughout the season. Ideally, water plants at ground level rather than overhead.

Types of marigolds: African marigold (*T. erecta*)—really from Mexico, 1' to 3' tall, large flowers that look like carnations, set 18" apart; French marigold (*T. patula*)—6" to 18" tall, single or double flowers smaller than African marigolds, triple types never set seed so bloom constantly, set 8" apart; Signet marigold (*T. tenuifolia*)—6" to 8" tall, soft lacy, ferny, lemon-scented foliage, small flowers edible on salads.

Potential problems: slugs and Japanese beetles might be problems, although healthy marigolds are rarely troubled by pests or diseases.

BRAZILIAN VERBENA, TALL VERBENA
Verbena bonariensis
Category: flowering tender perennial
Uses: massed or scattered throughout borders, in butterfly gardens
Soil: well-drained, moist
Hardiness: zones 6 to 10
Mature size: 4' to 6' tall, 1' to 2' wide

Brazilian verbena is a long-blooming tender perennial that self-sows in most gardens. Those seedlings produce strong-growing, drought-resistant plants. Brazilian verbena's cheerful purple flowers cluster on narrow, airy, almost leafless deep green 4' to 6' tall rough-textured square stems that branch frequently and move gracefully with a small breeze. They can be massed in a border and can even be used in the middle or front of the border as the plants have such a soft and airy nature; think of a see-through curtain or veil of purple. That light nature is why Brazilian verbena will not work as a backdrop but is best mixed with other plants and is very effective with contrasting yellow and orange blooms or blending with pink shades. It is a rewarding in a cottage garden and will attract as many butterflies and other insects as the butterfly bush.

In spring, transplant container-grown specimens into the garden, or start seed in containers about eight weeks prior to the last frost date or outside in well-prepared soil as spring warms. Seeds and seedlings need to be kept adequately moist for good growth and will bloom the first year. Brazilian verbena will thrive in well-drained soil with some organic matter added, but resent "wet feet" or soggy soil. It is quite drought tolerant once fully established. Fertilize once in spring or add a time-release fertilizer. If you grow Brazilian verbena in full sun, the plants will stand up well without additional support, unlike most tall growing plants.

Potential problems: Brazilian verbena has few insect and disease problems other than powdery mildew.

PANSY
Viola x *wittrockiana*
Category: flowering annual
Use: in borders, edges, containers, and window boxes
Soil: moist, fertile, well-drained
Hardiness: annual in New England
Mature size: 6" to 8" tall, a bit less wide

Pansies are wonderfully diverse cool-season plants with blue, red, rose, purple, yellow, and white 2" to 4" flowers often with stripes, blotches, and "happy faces." They make brightly colored beds and edgings when massed, and also work well in containers and window boxes. Early spring bulbs can be interplanted in beds. Flowers can be cut for cheerful small arrangements.

Choose from the diverse selection of container-grown plants available very early and plant as soon as soil can be worked. Space plants about 4" to 6" apart in fertile, moist, well-drained

ABOVE: Brazilian verbena (*Verbena bonariensis*)
BELOW: Pansy (*Viola* x *wittrockiana*)

soil in the sun or partial shade. To prolong flowering, mulch plants with organic matter to keep roots cool; keep well watered and regularly fertilized; remove spent flowers for longer bloom. Seed should be sown about eight to ten weeks prior to your planting-out date. Early fall planting of pansies is also successful in many areas; they will flower and be well established prior to frost. Many varieties work for fall planting, although the 'Icicle' pansies are specifically selected to withstand a lot of cold.

Varieties include: 'Antique Shades'—soft, muted shades of apricot to rose, orange blotches, 3" flowers; 'Bingo' series—upward facing 3 ½" flowers, solid colors; 'Crystal Bowl' series—clear, solid colors, 2 ½" wide, 7" tall; 'Jolly Jokers'—bright, mostly orange and purple, 3" "faces"; All American Selection' 'Icicle' series—clear shades and blotched, blue, orange, white, and almost black; 'Imperial' series—bicolor and pastels, 3 ½" flowers, 6" tall.

Potential problems: mildew and slugs can occasionally be problems.

Lamb's ears and 'Purple Rain' salvia are attractive plants that deer rarely eat.

■ Troubleshooting in the Garden

In Northeast gardens, there are some problems with pests and diseases, although most will be avoided if you grow healthy plants. Grow your plants in healthy, organic soil. Even plants that grow naturally in lean and very well-drained soils are unhappy in nutrient-deprived soils; the better the soil, the better the plants. Plants that are vigorous and healthy look attractive, flower or fruit well, and have the fewest problems.

Put the right plant in the right place. Regardless of a plant's needs, if you "stretch" the rules too far, you will create a challenge for that plant. A plant that is not doing well is susceptible to disease and pests. You should plant shade plants in the shade and sun lovers in the sun; group plants with similar needs together. Do not try combining a desert plant and a bog plant in the same area of your garden; one or both will be unhappy. Giving a plant what it wants will go a long way toward your goal of maintaining a healthy garden.

Proper watering is also critical to plant health. Provide the proper amount of water that each plant needs. It's best to water early in the day so plants can dry off before nightfall; plants with wet leaves at night are more at risk for disease. Watering during the coolest part of the day will keep evaporation at a minimum and preserve our resources. Do not forget to water evergreen plants through dry times in fall and winter (until the ground freezes); they still have leaves and need water. Water the soil rather than the plants. This gets the water where it is needed, prevents evaporation, and keeps water off the leaves.

Mulching improves plants' chances of survival and the odds they will thrive. Mulch helps maintain soil temperatures, keep soil moist, prevent weeds from growing, and prevent water splashing onto leaves from the ground, which in turn prevents disease. Slugs can be attracted to the moisture and warmth mulch holds, but can be dealt with by using traps or baits. Mulch improves soil and moisture conditions, which help plants stay healthy. Preventing the growth of weeds improves your odds of maintaining healthy plants as weeds often harbor insects and diseases.

Choose disease-resistant plants for your garden. As you learn more about your own garden and gardens in your area, you will discover that some plants just do not do well where you live. Those plants should be avoided as they will always be weak growers, which attract pests and diseases. Some plants are hybridized to resist certain diseases; choose those when you can.

A neat and tidy garden is attractive, and a healthier growing environment. Regularly remove debris and litter, along with damaged leaves. Your garden will look better and you will have fewer problems. If you have a badly diseased plant or one covered with pests, consider getting rid of it. Put it in the garbage, not the compost pile. Doing so will ensure that plant will no longer be able to spread problems and make the situation worse.

If you grow vegetables, grow them in small, scattered patches rather than one large one. This will help prevent the spread of pests and diseases. Move crops from year to year; for instance, do not regularly plant tomatoes in the same soil. Diseases can accumulate in that soil.

Buy only healthy, vigorous growing plants; do not bring home a problem. A healthy plant should be covered with leaves of good color and, if it's flowering season, a good number of flowers and buds. Many discolored leaves or deformed flowers are the signs of a sick plant. Pests should not be crawling on or jumping from leaves. Run your fingers over the top and bottom of the leaves, testing for sticky areas, a gritty feel, or small pests themselves. Avoid purchasing plants with those symptoms. Roots should not be pushing up out of the soil and growing out the bottom of the pot in large numbers. This pot-bound condition makes the plant a challenge to handle.

In your garden, learn to be tolerant of some damage; nature is about give and take. A small number of pests will do little damage, and if you spray to eliminate them, you also will eliminate the beneficial insects that help control the problem naturally. With healthy plants and practices, your garden is likely to remain stable and without lots of pests and diseases.

PREVENTING AND CONTROLLING DISEASES

Healthy plants are far less likely to be challenged by disease. Select hybrids and types of plants that are less susceptible to disease; catalogs and labels will indicate that attribute. Avoid overcrowding plants; plants need space to do well and for air to circulate. Plant them far enough apart and make sure you do not block air flow with too many walls, hedges, or other hardscape features. Avoid walking through wet plants and into another section of the garden, which can spread disease.

Mulch is terrific for many reasons. Follow the guidelines in the mulch section for correct depth; you need enough, but not too much. Do not pile it against the stems of plants or do "volcano" mulching of trees and shrubs. Be diligent about removing any diseased plant or its leaves from the garden and do not compost this material. Once you have handled diseased material, wash your hands to avoid spreading problems.

Once you see any problem—basically a plant that does not look as it should, often one that is not growing vigorously any more—investigate what is causing it. Use reference books or consult your local extension office or master gardeners for help. Do not just guess at the problem and start spraying and hoping for the best. Knowledge of the specific problem will lead you to the best solution.

The two biggest disease problems ornamental gardeners have are powdery mildew (a white, powdery appearance that covers leaves); and black spot (discoloration and loss of leaves, especially of roses). For both, spray with baking soda or fungicide and keep the garden clean of diseased leaves and plants. You can also avoid the problem by planting more disease-resistant hybrids.

A FEW COMMON PESTS OF ORNAMENTAL PLANTS

The following are some pests you may find in your garden:

Aphids—tiny, pear-shaped insects with soft bodies that leave a sticky substance on leaves; spray off with a hose, use summer oil spray or insecticidal soap, or release beneficial insects such as ladybird beetles or lacewings.

Black vine weevil—1" to 2" long beetle you rarely see that makes notches in rhododendron leaves and others; control with beneficial nematodes.

Caterpillars—larvae of moths and butterflies, they eat many leaves but often turn into attractive butterflies; learn which are which.

Japanese beetles—1½" long, metallic blue-green beetles that eat many plants (their larvae are destructive grubs in soil); use milky spore for lawns, handpick beetles at night, and drown them in soapy water or spray them with neem. Do not use Japanese beetle traps, which attract your neighbors' beetles over for a snack.

Slugs—slimy snails without shells; control with organic slug bait or beer in shallow containers set at ground level.

Whiteflies—tiny white flies that fly when you bump or shake a plant; use yellow sticky traps, insecticidal soap, or summer oil spray.

ACTION STEPS AGAINST PESTS

■ Identify the insect to determine if it is a pest

■ Study your garden to determine how many there are and in which areas

■ Spray the plant(s) with water under enough pressure to wash pests off plant

■ Handpick pests if appropriate

■ If a single plant is inundated with pests, destroy it or cut it back near the ground

■ Spray with the following low-toxicity organic pesticides:

DORMANT OIL—a heavy oil that is sprayed on deciduous woody plants in late winter; smothers larvae and eggs

INSECTICIDAL SOAP—the salts of fatty acids applied as spray to kill small soft-bodied insects

NEEM—low-toxicity spray from neem tree in India

SUMMER OIL SPRAY (ultrafine oil)—highly refined oil that can be sprayed while plants are in growth, smothers insects (do not confuse with dormant oil) ■

PESTICIDE SAFETY

When you spray anything in your garden, even organic sprays, it is imperative that you follow all safety rules. Always read the label and follow the instructions; never use more than it says to use. Keep pesticides in original containers and locked up for safety. Do not smoke or eat while working with them and do not spray on a windy day; wait for the wind to stop blowing. Follow temperature guidelines for each product, but never spray above 80 degrees Fahrenheit. Wear protective gear or clothing, which should be washed separately and immediately after use. Then clean your wash machine by running an additional wash cycle with nothing in it. Do not dump any chemical down your drain, sewer, or behind the garage. Dispose of chemicals at your local hazardous waste dump, along with empty pesticide containers, on specified days for hazardous materials.

WEED PREVENTION AND CONTROL

Weeds are unattractive (mostly) and fight with the ornamental plants for water and nutrients. They have terrific survival strategies, so continued effort and vigilance is critical to winning the battle. Weeds produce copious quantities of seed—so never let them go to seed, which will spread all over your garden. Also, never add weed seeds to your compost pile. Avoid buying bird seed with high weed seed content.

Pull weeds regularly; it's easiest when the ground is moist from a recent rain. Grasp the stem close to the ground and pull. Try to dig out as much of the weed's root as possible. Often only a small piece of root left behind is enough for it to grow back. Just keep at it. The weed will be weaker with each successive generation.

In gravel driveways, walkways, and sidewalk cracks, use a garden flame thrower or propane torch to singe the plants, which damages them so they die.

Try to avoid tilling regularly, which turns the weed seeds near the surface of the soil so they germinate. Covering an area prior to planting with a thick mulch of paper, cardboard, or black plastic can kill weeds.

Solarization will kill weeds prior to planting. Remove surface weeds and turn soil over in the desired area, then saturate with water. The next day cover with clear, heavy, 3 to 6 mil plastic, with the edges buried. Four weeks will kill most weeds; however, a lawn will take up to three months. Once plastic is removed, you can work and plant the area after a few days.

DEER PROBLEMS AND MANAGEMENT

As the population of deer increases and predators decrease, they have become a large problem for gardeners. We are building more houses in former open and wild areas, giving the deer less room, just as their numbers grow. They are a difficult challenge.

Where the deer population is reasonable, gardeners can select plants that are less desirable to deer. Pungent and medicinal herbs or poisonous plants are less likely to be eaten, though there are no guarantees. However, poisonous plants are a concern for those with children and pets, so take measures necessary to protect them. When deer food supplies are low, in early spring and late winter, deer are likely to eat anything.

There are many repellants and deterrents that some gardeners say work for them. They all work best in areas with low population pressure, and also if it does not rain immediately after applying them. Commercial sprays, egg sprays, human hair and urine, soap hung in trees, and hot pepper sprays all work to some degree. Follow directions carefully; reapply about every ten days and after rain and rotate different approaches and products.

Fencing is the best approach where local zoning laws allow. An 8' high fence (10' is better in difficult areas) of heavy black plastic or metal is reasonably effective. The plastic will work unless deer are running into it because of panic; when that happens, it will give way.

COLD AND SNOW

There are special challenges for those growing in very cold and snowy climates. Even those who live in warmer areas will have cold microclimates in their gardens. Winter wind quickly desiccates broad-leaved evergreens; add winter sun and it spells trouble for many plants.

Creating Windbreaks

Plant a dense windbreak of plants or build a fence to slow the wind and blasts of cold air from buffeting your house and decrease damage to plants. The windbreak should be between the prevailing wind and the items protected. The most effective windbreaks are dense, not solid or open, and work best within a distance two to three times the height of the windbreak. Windbreaks on the top of a hill protect the area below.

A windbreak of evergreen trees planted on the north side on your property will help protect your house and plants and save on winter heating costs. Leave the south side open to receive the maximum winter sun.

DEER-RESISTANT PLANTS

BULBS:
Muscari spp. (grape hyacinth)
Narcissus spp. (daffodil)

GROUND COVERS:
Epimedium spp. (barrenwort)
Asarum spp. (wild ginger)

PERENNIALS:
Achillea spp. (yarrow)
Digitalis spp. (foxglove)
Echinacea spp. (coneflower)
Helleborus spp. (hellebore)
Salvia spp. (sage)
Stachys spp. (lamb's ears)
Thymus spp. (thyme)

SHRUBS (DECIDUOUS):
Buddleia davidii (butterfly bush)
Cotinus spp. (smoke bush)

Daphne spp. (garland flower)
Myrica pensylvanica (bayberry)
Syringa vulgaris (lilac)

TREES (DECIDUOUS):
Amelanchier spp. (shadblow)
Betula nigra (river birch)
Cornus spp. (dogwood)
Pyrus spp. (pear)
Rhus spp. (sumac)

EVERGREENS:
Buxus spp. (boxwood)
Cryptomeria japonica (Japanese cedar)
Ilex opaca (American holly)
Mahonia spp. (grape holly)
Microbiota decussata (Russian cypress)
Pieris japonica (Japanese pieris)
Taxus cuspidate (Japanese yew)

This soft, fluffy snow will not damage plants, but will give the gardener the opportunity to look at the "bones" of the garden and think about structural improvements.

Wrapping Plants for Winter Protection

Wet snow is heavy and can break upright branches of conifers. Wrap the shrub or tree with spiraling twine. You also can wrap the plant with burlap, then tie it by spiraling twine around the plant. You also can build a burlap "tent"; use bamboo stakes pulled together over the top of the plant, then wrap it in burlap and tie it with twine. The burlap could also be attached permanently to the stakes with rust-proof nails for use again in future years.

Winter Mulch

Mulch works to keep soil temperatures from fluctuating wildly. In winter, mulch applied after freezing temperatures helps keep the ground frozen and helps prevent freeze/thaw cycles, which can cause plants to heave out of the ground by pushing the plants, roots and all, to the surface of the soil. Apply 4" to 6" of organic mulch, compost, or straw after the ground freezes. The mulch should cover the rootzone, but not be up against the stems or trunks of plants. This also works with a plant that is "borderline" hardy (a gardener's little white lie to himself about the hardiness of a plant). The mulch will help prevent the plant from dying because of excessive cold.

Winterize Your Plants

Help your plants get ready for winter by keeping them in the best health possible. Give them adequate water through the growing season into fall up to frost. If it does not rain during this time, supplement by watering. Do not prune or fertilize woody plants in the fall, as that will encourage new growth. That growth will be tender and probably die when hit with the freezing temperatures of winter. For similar reasons, do not plant later than six weeks before frost. Plants will not have had time for roots to grow and for above-ground tissue to "harden off," which enables the plant to fend off the cold.

Cold-Tolerant Plants

Select plants that are rated cold hardy for your growing zone to help ensure they survive and thrive. Search for short-season vegetables that grow to maturity with a minimum of growing days. Be aware of what other gardeners are growing well in your area. Find quality local nurseries that understand your special challenges, as most mail-order nurseries sell throughout the United States and may only have a few plants suited for your area. It is also good to purchase plants grown locally, because they are certain to be hardier than one from an area some distance away, particularly a warmer climate.

The following are very cold-tolerant perennials good for Zone 3 winters and cold micro-climates:

Achillea spp. (yarrow)
Aruncus dioicus (goat's beard)
Bergenia cordifolia (heart-leaf pigsqueak)
Campanula spp. (bellflower)
Convallaria majalis (lily-of-the-valley)
Dicentra spp. (bleeding heart)
Filipendula (meadowsweet)
Hemerocallis (daylily)
Hosta spp. (hosta)
Lamium spp. (dead-nettle)
Nepeta spp. (catmint)
Phlox spp. (phlox)
Rudbeckia fulgida (black-eyed Susan)
Veronica incana (woolly speedwell)

Aquilegia spp. (columbine)
Baptisia australis (false indigo)
Brunnera macrophylla (borage)
Cerastium tomentosum (snow-in-summer)
Coreopsis verticillata (thread-leaf coreopsis)
Echinacea purpurea (purple coneflower)
Gypsophila paniculata (baby's breath)
Heuchera sanguinea (coral bells)
Iris spp. (iris)
Lysimachia clethroides (gooseneck loosestrife)
Papaver spp. (poppy)
Pulmonaria spp. (lungwort)
Sedum spp. (stonecrop)
Veronica spicata (spike speedwell)

Extending the Season

Most season-extending techniques have been developed by vegetable growers seeking to extend the harvest or begin it earlier than others. These approaches, all about temperature manipulation, have to do with keeping the cold air away from the plants or warming soil up early in the season.

A simple and inexpensive product to use is a garden fabric row cover. These are made to be water and sun permeable and keep the plants warmer than air temperature. You can hold the fabric in a tunnel shape over your plants by making wire arches or purchasing similar items. That fabric tunnel allows you to plant seedlings out earlier in the spring and keep plants going longer in the fall. Hot caps and glass cloches cover individual plants and function similarly. Cold frames are low rectangular structures made with glass or plastic tops to allow sunlight in like short, small greenhouses. A greenhouse is the most permanent way to extend your season, but also the most expensive.

There are heavier-weight insulators for short-term use, including a blanket-like cover called a garden quilt. Sometimes old blankets can serve the same purpose. These can be used to cover plants when very cold temperatures are forecast for a single night or for a few nights. This will keep plants alive a few days or weeks longer into the season.

Soil can be warmed early in the season by using black plastic mulch. Once the soil is at planting temperature, you can plant right through it by cutting a planting hole. Add the row cover over the top, and plants will grow quickly.

Seaside Conditions

The seacoast of the Northeast is a natural marvel. It also offers unique growing conditions not found elsewhere. The soil is sandy and salty and is not moisture retentive. Air is humid, sometimes foggy, and moves in salt-laden wind. Light varies from fog-shrouded to intense, human-crisping sun. Plants need to be tough to survive these conditions. Some plants proven to do well in various zones along the sea include:

Perennials

Artemisia stelleriana (beach wormwood)
Cerastium tomentosum (snow-in-summer)
Eschscholzia californica (California poppy)
Hemerocallis (daylily)
Lychnis coronaria (rose campion)
Veronica spp. (speedwell)

Asclepias tuberosa (butterfly weed)
Dianthus spp. (pinks)
Gypsophila paniculata (baby's breath)
Iberis sempervirens (candytuft)
Sedum spp. (stonecrop)

Shrubs

Clethra alnifolia (summersweet)
Cytisus scoparius (scotch broom)
Myrica pensylvanica (bayberry)
Rhus spp. (sumac)
Sambucus canadensis (elderberry)
Tamarix spp. (tamarisk)

Cornus sericea (American dogwood)
Hydrangea macrophylla (hydrangea)
Pinus mugo (mugo pine)
Rosa wichuraiana (memorial rose)
Syringa vulgaris (lilac)

Trees

Aesculus hippocastanum (horse chestnut)
Cryptomeria japonica (Japanese cedar)
Pinus rigida (pitch pine)
Quercus alba (white oak)
Ulmus parvifolia (Chinese elm)

Amelanchier canadensis (shadbush)
Nyssa sylvatica (tupelo)
Pinus thunbergii (Japanese black pine)
Thuja occidentalis (white cedar)

Resources

NURSERIES

A special thanks to Ruah Donnelly for her knowledge and for her book, *The Adventurous Gardener: Where to Buy the Best Plants in New England* (The Horticultural Press, 2000), which was invaluable in compiling this list.

Oliver Nurseries, Inc.
1159 Bronson Rd.
Fairfield, CT 06430
203-259-5609

Sam Bridge Nursery & Greenhouse
437 North St.
Greenwich, CT 06830
203-869-3418

Twombly Nursery
163 Barn Hill Rd.
Monroe, CT 06468
203-261-2133

Fieldstone Gardens
55 Quaker Lane
Vassalboro, ME 04989-3816
207-923-3836

O'Donal's Nurseries
6 County Rd., RFD 4 (Rtes. 114 and 22)
Gorham, ME 04038
207-839-4262

Plainview Farm
529 Mountfort Rd.
North Yarmouth, ME 04097
207-829-5004, 800-396-1705

Briggs Nursery
295 Kelley Blvd.
North Attleboro, MA 02760-4194
508-699-7421

Mahoney's Garden Center
242 Cambridge St. (Rte. 3)
Winchester, MA 01890
781-729-5900

Russell's Garden Center
397 Boston Post Rd. (Rte. 20)
Wayland, MA 01778
508-358-2283

Weston Nurseries
93 E. Main St. (Rte. 135)
Hopkinton, MA 01748-0186
508-435-3414

Andrew's Greenhouse
1230 S. East St.
Amherst, MA 01002
413-253-2937

Hadley Garden Center
285 Russell St.
Hadley, MA 01373
413-584-1423

Windy Hill Farm
686 Stockbridge Rd. (Rte. 7)
Great Barrington, MA 01230
413-298-3217

Bakers' Acres
1104 Auburn Rd. (Rte. 34)
Groton, NY 13073
607-533-4653

Masterson's Aquatic Nursery and Water Garden Center
725 Olean Rd.
East Aurora, NY 14052-9781
716-655-0133

Rosedale Nurseries, Inc
Saw Mill River Rd. (Rte. 9A)
Hawthorne, NY 10532-1598
914-769-1300

Sprainbrook Nursery, Inc.
448 Underhill Rd.
Scarsdale, NY 10583
914-723-2382

Matterhorn Nursery
227 Summit Park Rd.
Spring Valley, NY 10977
845-354-5986

The Bayberry
50 Montauk Hwy.
Amagansett, NY 11937
631-267-3000

Hicks Nurseries, Inc.
100 Jericho Turnpike
Westbury, NY 11590
516-334-0066

Marders Nursery
Snake Hollow Rd.
Bridgehampton, NY 11932
631-537-3700

Lake Street Garden Center
37 Lake St.
Salem, NH 03079-2243
603-893-5858

Rolling Green Nursery
64 Breakfast Hill Rd.
Greenland, NH 03840
603-436-2732

Dilatush Nursery
148 Larrison Rd.
Wrightstown, NJ 08691-2002
608-585-8696

Rappleyea's Nursery
523A Chesterfield Arneytown Rd.
Allentown, NJ 08501
609-298-2450

Horsford Gardens and Nursery
2111 Greenbush Rd. (Rte. 7)
Charlotte, VT 05445
802-425-2811

Rocky Dale Gardens
62 Rocky Dale Rd. (Rte. 116)
Bristol, VT 05443
802-453-2782

MAIL-ORDER SUPPLIERS

Please note that many of the suppliers who ship catalogs free in the U.S. charge a fee for shipment to Canada. Also, most suppliers have on-line catalogs.

THE SYMBOLS BELOW INDICATE OFFERINGS:

(P) PLANTS

(S) SEED

(B) BULBS

($0.00) CATALOG PRICE ON PUBLICATION

Appalachian Gardens (P) free
P.O. Box 82
Waynesboro, PA 17268-0082
717-762-4312

Bluestone Perennials (P) free
7211 Middle Ridge Rd.
Madison, OH 44057-3096
800-852-5243
www.bluestoneperennials.com

Brent and Becky's Bulbs (B) free
7900 Daffodil Lane
Gloucester, VA 23061
804-693-3966
www.brentandbeckysbulbs.com

W. Atlee Burpee & Co. (S) free
300 Park Ave.
Warminster, PA 18974-0001
800-333-5808
www.burpee.com

Busse Gardens (P) $3.00
17160 245th Ave.
Big Lake, MN 55309
800-544-3192
www.bussegardens.com

Forestfarm (P) free
990 Tetherow Rd.
Williams, OR 97544-9599
541-846-7269
www.forestfarm.com

Goodwin Creek Gardens (P) free with purchase
P.O. Box 83
Williams, OR 97544
800-846-7359
www.goodwincreekgardens.com

Greer Gardens (P) free
1280 Goodpasture Island Rd.
Eugene, OR 97401-1794
800-548-0111
www.greergardens.com

Gossler Farms Nursery (P) free
1200 Weaver Rd.
Springfield, OR 97478-9691
541-746-3922
www.gosslerfarms.com

Heronswood Nursery Ltd. (P) $5.00
7530 N.E. 288th St.
Kingston, WA 98346
360-297-4172
www.heronswood.com

J. L. Hudson, Seedsman (S) free
Star Route 2, Box 337
La Honda CA 94020-9733
www.jhudsonseeds.net

Johnny's Selected Seeds (S) free
955 Benton Ave.
Winslow, ME 04901
800-879-2258
www.johnnyseeds.com

Klehm's Song Sparrow Farm & Nursery (P) free
4210 N. Duncan Rd.
Champaign, IL 61821
800-553-3715
www.klehm.com

Lilypons Water Gardens (P) $5.00
P.O. Box 10
Buckeystown, MD 21717-0010
800-999-5459
www.lilypons.com

Miller. Nurseries (P) free
5060 West Lake Rd.
Canandaigua, NY 14424-8904
800-836-9630
www.millernurseries.com

Niche Gardens (P) $3.00
1111 Dawson Rd.
Chapel Hill, NC 27516
919-967-0078
www.nichegardens.com

Nichols Garden Nursery (S) free
1190 Old Salem Rd. N.E.
Albany, OR 97321-4580
800-422-3985
www.nicholsgardennursery.com

Park Seed (S) free
1 Parkton Ave.
Greenwood, SC 29647-0001
800-213-0076
www.parkseed.com

Pinetree Garden Seeds (S) free
P.O. Box 300
New Gloucester, ME 04260
207-926-3400
www.superseeds.com

Plant Delights Nursery (P) free
9241 Sauls Road
Raleigh, NC 27603
919-772-4794
www.plantdelights.com

Richters (P) free
357 Hwy. 47
Goodwood, Ontario
L0C 1A0 Canada
905-640-6677
www.richters.com

Roses of Yesterday (P) $5.00
803 Brown's Valley Rd.
Watsonville, CA 95076-0398
831-728-1901
www.rosesofyesterday.com

Roslyn Nursery (P) free
211 Burrs Lane
Dix Hills, NY 11746
631-643-9347
www.roslynnursery.com

Select Seeds (S) free
180 Stickney Hill Rd.
Union, CT 06076-4617
800-684-0395
www.selectseeds.com

Schipper & Co. U.S.A. (B) free
P.O. Box 7584
Greenwich, CT 06836
888-847-8637
www.colorblends.com

Stokes Seed (S) free
P.O. Box 548
Buffalo, NY 14240-0548
905-688-4300 or 716-695-6980
www.stokeseed.com

Tranquil Lake Nursery (P) $1.00
45 River St.
Rehoboth, MA 02769-1395
508-252-4002
www.tranquil-lake.com

Wayside Gardens (P) free
1 Garden Lane
Hodges, SC 29695-0001
800-213-0379
www.waysidegardens.com

EXTENSION SERVICES

Search for local programs on the Urban Programs Resource Networks site:
http://www.urbanext.uiuc.edu/netlinks/ces.html

Cornell Cooperative Extension, Cornell University: www.cce.cornell.edu

Rutgers Cooperative Extension, Rutgers University: www.rce.rutgers.edu

UMassExtension, University of Massachusetts: www.umassextension.org

University of Maine Cooperative Extension: www.umext.maine.edu/

SUGGESTED READING

Donnelly, Ruah, *The Adventurous Gardener: Where to Buy the Best Plants in New England* (The Horticultural Press, 2000).

Gardner, Jigs, and Jo Ann, *Gardens of Use & Delight: Uniting the Practical and Beautiful in an Integrated Landscape* (Fulcrum Publishing, 2002).

Halpin, Anne, ed., *Northeastern Garden Book* (Sunset Publishing Corporation, 2001).

Karlin, Lynn, and Rebecca Sawyer-Fay, *Gardens Maine Style* (Down East Books, 2001).

Lanza, Patricia, *Lasagna Gardening: A New Layering System for Bountiful Gardens: No Digging, No Tilling, No Weeding, No Kidding!* (Rodale Books, 1999).

Index

NOTE: page numbers in italics indicate illustrations.